KU-016-677

COMMISSIONER CATHERINE

Catherine Bramwell-Booth
with
Ted Harrison

Darton, Longman and Todd
London

First published in 1983 by
Darton, Longman and Todd Ltd
89 Lillie Road, London SW6 1UD

Reprinted 1983

© 1983 Catherine Bramwell-Booth and Ted Harrison

ISBN 0 232 51589 1

British Library Cataloguing in Publication Data

Bramwell-Booth, Catherine
  Commissioner Catherine.
  1. Bramwell-Booth, Catherine
  I. Title
  267'.15'0924   BX9743.B/

ISBN 0–232–51589–1

Phototypeset by Input Typesetting Ltd, London SW19 8DR
Printed in Great Britain by The Anchor Press Ltd
and bound by Wm Brendon & Son Ltd
both of Tiptree, Essex.

Contents

Acknowledgements

Thanks are due to The Salvation Army for permission to reproduce extracts from *No Discharge in This War* by General Frederick Coutts; also to the following for permission to reproduce illustrations from copyright sources: Doug Mackenzie (p.viii), BBC Hulton Picture Library, (p.23) and Keystone Press Agency (p.112).

Introduction

As a retired Salvation Army officer in her nineties, Commissioner Catherine Bramwell-Booth probably spoke to more people than her grandfather ever did—in all his missions, open-air meetings and great speaking tours put together. And what is more, Commissioner Catherine seldom had to leave her Berkshire home to do this, and if she did she travelled no farther than London.

She was born into an age when the letter and telegram were the fastest means of communication. The wireless and television were yet to be invented. Road transport moved at the speed of the horse. Yet, in her hundredth year she appeared effortlessly to have mastered all the devices of twentieth-century mass communication, undreamt of in her youth. She could hold a television or radio audience in the way that her grandfather could hold the attention of a public meeting. She used charm and humour but made no concessions to modern queasiness in tackling individual spiritual matters with great directness.

Sitting prim in her navy Salvation Army uniform in a modern television studio under the harsh studio lights she was in charge, not the interviewer, the floor manager or the director. She dictated the pace of events and refused to be overawed by the electronic hardware around her and the jargon of the production team. By unconsciously breaking the rules and conventions of modern television production, the Commissioner created memorable programmes and became a much-loved figure.

Television appearances were comparatively rare compared with the interviews she gave in her own home to radio and newspaper journalists. They would typically be asked to arrive at 11 o'clock in the morning and would be welcomed by the Commissioner's sister, Colonel Olive. Major Dora would bring coffee into a downstairs sitting-room.

The three sisters, aged from ninety upwards, live together with a cook in a large Victorian house in the Berkshire countryside. It is approached down a tree-lined drive, and to arrive at the front door is like being taken back in time, seventy years at least. In the hall, a dark inner hall, is a great Salvation Army drum and a bust of their father, General Bramwell Booth. The sitting room is furnished in a comfortable, ageless manner. There are water-colours on the wall and potted plants. Coffee is taken with Colonel Olive. Talk is of the garden. It is only when modern topics of conversation are raised that the spell is broken. The sisters keep well abreast of current affairs, and Colonel Olive's sharp mind and practical opinions are not to be underestimated.

In due course the Commissioner arrives, in uniform. The first thing one notices about her is how straight she stands. The next thing one notices is her clear and very precise way of talking. As soon as the interview is to start her sisters, and perhaps other Salvationists who may be present, are gently asked to leave. As the interview proceeds the Commissioner becomes as much interested in the visitor as he or she is in the stories the Commissioner has to tell. She wants to know about the visitor's family, religious convictions, if any, ambitions and hopes. The interview is punctuated by a chiming clock and comes to an end when the bell for lunch is heard. Lunch is a light but formal meal. All their life the sisters have been largely vegetarian, eating only fish or poultry occasionally. After lunch the interview may continue, but normally the Commissioner needs to rest.

This book is compiled from transcripts of a series of such interviews recorded during the Commissioner's one hundredth year. To set the extracts in context the book starts with a brief history of The Salvation Army, and each chapter draws on the Commissioner's own writings, notably her lives of her father and grandmother. The book is a series of memories of people, places and events known to Commissioner Catherine. It contains her reflections on life and certain insights into her faith and struggle to keep her faith. It is not a biography but an introduction to and meeting with a remarkable person and a remarkable family.

Commissioner Catherine Bramwell-Booth at her home in Berkshire in her hundredth year.

The Early Days

To some, The Salvation Army is all tambourines and brass bands. To others, The Salvation Army is a bed for the night, a refuge from the streets. To many, The Salvation Army is a pretty girl in an old-fashioned bonnet going the rounds of the pubs and bars selling newspapers. To thousands, The Salvation Army has been a personal turning-point from despair to hope. To Catherine Bramwell-Booth, The Salvation Army has been her life.

From the vantage point of her one hundredth year and as granddaughter of the founder and daughter of the second Salvation Army general, Catherine Bramwell-Booth combines both a historical over-view and an intimate knowledge of the Army's development. Important events she did not witness first-hand she heard about from those who did.

The story of The Salvation Army begins with the story of a romance, a love affair between a tall, earnest pawnbroker and the rather delicate daughter of a Derbyshire coachbuilder, the pawnbroker being William Booth and the coachbuilder's daughter Catherine Mumford.

Catherine Mumford was a determined and radical Christian. Born in Derbyshire but brought up in Lincolnshire, she had moved with her parents to London at the age of sixteen. Long periods of illness had given her time to read and consider her thoughts and she developed strong, well-reasoned views. Before meeting William Booth she had set out the essential prerequisites in the man she would take as a husband:

He must be a sincere Christian; not a nominal one, or a

mere church member, but truly converted to God. I resolved that he should be a man of sense. I knew that I could never respect a fool, or one much weaker mentally than myself. . . . Another resolution I made was that I would never marry a man who was not a total abstainer, and this from conviction and not merely to gratify me.

Unessential, but desirable, Catherine Mumford considered that he should be a minister: 'I could be most useful to God as a minister's wife.' And she added, 'He should be dark, tall and for preference called William!'

William Booth was born in Nottingham in the same year as Catherine, 1829. He was converted at the age of fifteen, and one of his first practical deeds as a Christian was to scandalize his local Methodist congregation by marching his first ragged regiment into the best pews at the Wesley Chapel in his home town. He was reprimanded and told that in future his outcasts were to enter by a side door and remain out of sight during the service.

At the age of nineteen William Booth moved to London to take up a job in a pawnbroker's shop. He worked long hours and the little spare time he had was devoted to preaching. His father, a speculative builder, had made and lost a fortune by the time William was twelve, and so from an early age he learned about the struggles of life. As a young apprentice in Nottingham William had been greatly impressed by the Chartist orator Feargus O'Connor when he had visited the city propounding his Reformist creed. He had also heard the American Methodist spellbinder James Caughey preaching. The seeds for the great socially reforming Christian movement were sown early.

In London the seeds began to develop. He joined the Reformers within the Methodist Church and much impressed a wealthy businessman, Mr Edward Rabbits, who heard him preach. Mr Rabbits was a friend of Catherine Mumford and her mother and when William was invited to preach at the chapel which they attended, Catherine observed that the young preacher's sermon had been the best she had heard there. The next day William Booth and Catherine Mumford met at tea at Mr Rabbits' house. She took his side in a discussion with those present on the subject of drink and total abstention.

William was able to leave his job at the pawnbroker's shop when Mr Rabbits offered to support him financially for three months as an evangelist. A little later Mr Rabbits insisted that William come with him to one of the Reformer's meetings in a schoolroom off the City Road in London. There he met Catherine Mumford again. He accompanied her home and the journey proved to be one of great significance. Their granddaughter was later to describe it in this way:

> Side by side she and William sit. The carriage rattles over the unpaved road. First from one side, then from the other, dim light from without spreads brief shadowy glimmer through the dusk within as they drive past the small pools of light round the street lamps. Remarks are made, their voices surprisingly sound normal! But presently each in secret realizes that this is a moment apart, a moment to be remembered for ever. The little space they occupy is suddenly illumined, and these two see one another; see one another—and know! From inside the closed carriage, travelling through the darkening streets, each looks up, and, like Jacob after the sun had set on that other evening long ago, sees heaven brought within reach of earth. Oblivious of their situation, each knows 'The Lord is in this place.' Yes! Neither of them ever doubts that.

William wrote it was God himself '. . . Who in a most wonderful and providential manner has brought us together, and then flashed into our hearts the sweet and heavenly feeling of a something more than earthly unison'. Nothing that happened to them afterwards had power to mar the gift, nor to tarnish the memory of the timeless moment when love made a shining pathway, from the carriage in which they sat, to heaven's gate: a pathway they would walk together. Catherine, as Mrs Booth, wrote long afterwards:

> That little journey will never be forgotten by either of us

. . . as William expressed it, 'it seemed as if God flashed simultaneously into our hearts that affection which. . . none of the changing vicissitudes with which our lives have been so crowded has been able to efface. . .We struck in at once in such wonderful harmony of view and aim and feeling on various matters that passed rapidly before us, that it seemed as though we had intimately known and loved each other for years and suddenly, after some temporary absence, had been brought together again.' Before we reached my home we both . . . felt as though we had been made for each other.

On their arrival, the talk continued. 'No doubt we drew each other out,' Catherine says. 'The conversation was lively and interesting, and my mother listened and had her say.'

Catherine, the Mother of The Salvation Army, was almost at the end of her life when she recorded this, but the scenes of that Good Friday evening were as clear as yesterday. In Mrs Mumford's presence, and though no word of love had been spoken, love bound the two young hearts as one, transmuted all their possessions into gifts for each other. Soon it was later than could be believed. Where was Mr Booth going? Catherine discovered 'he had purposed to stop at his cousin's. Instead of that he had got into this meeting and from this meeting had come on with me.' It was now far too late to walk to his cousin's and Mrs Mumford invited him to stay the night. Catherine and William parted with a formal handshake, the light of love shining on the brow of each as they stood smiling, fearless into the other's eyes.

There followed a period of heart-searching, especially on William's side. He only had the means of supporting himself for three months; how could he contemplate supporting a wife and family? He was bursting with a whole host of ambitious ideas to do God's work as he saw it; getting married had not entered his calculations at all until he met Catherine. And Catherine decreed that she would only accept William's love if he were convinced that he would be doing God's will by declaring it.

The Victorians were masters of the romantic letter and William and Catherine excelled in the genre. Between the formal opening 'My dear friend' and the restrained conclusion 'Yours affectionately' they poured out their deepest feelings both of joy and of despair. 'The more you lead me up to Christ', wrote Catherine, 'in all things, the more highly shall I esteem you, and if it be possible to love you more than I do now, the more shall I love you.'

I know not that I have anything to write about in any way cheering to your feelings. . . I fear I have blocked up for ever any possible way of being made a blessing to you. . . . Darkness gathers thicker than ever round the path I tread, and doubt, gloom, melancholy and despair would tread me down. My resolutions are unbroken to live and die only for the salvation of souls. . . I say nothing decisive, because I know nothing, I have neither advanced nor retrograded from the position I occupied when last we met,

wrote William in one of his moments of depression. Catherine challenged William to test his dilemma before God.

If you are satisfied of his will, irrespective of circumstances, let circumstances go and let us be one, come what will. . . . if you feel satisfied on these two points, first, that the step is not opposed to the will of God, and secondly that I am calculated to make you happy, come on Saturday evening and on our knees before God let us give ourselves afresh to him and to each other for his sake, consecrate our whole selves to his service, for Him to live and die.

William came. Hand in hand he and Catherine knelt and prayed. Nearly a year later she recalled the time.

We solemnly gave ourselves to each other and to God. We will always keep that day as our real wedding day. It was so in the sight of God and in all the highest and holiest senses, the next is a mere legal knot, that was a moral and spiritual union.

William and Catherine Booth at about the time of their marriage (1855).

Kneeling side by side, hand in hand to pray together, became a life-long custom. William and Catherine were married in London on 16 June 1855, some three years after first meeting.

The intervening three years were important to William in that they established his reputation as an evangelist. His three-month contract with Mr Rabbits was not renewed. He had to start selling his furniture to live, but despite the imminent threat of dire poverty, according to one story, William nevertheless gave his last sixpence to a poor widow.

But William's reputation as a preacher had reached Spalding in Lincolnshire and the local Reformers invited him to take charge of their circuit. He worked there for eighteen months, receiving almost daily letters from Catherine, some of them two and three thousand words long. Often she worried about his health and chided him for working too hard.

In 1854 he returned to London to study for the ministry of the Methodist New Connexion. He made such an impression that he was appointed resident minister at the new Packington Street chapel. He was also given permission to marry at the end of twelve months. Invitations to preach arrived from various parts of the country, so much so that he spent as much time in revival campaigns as in ministering to his London congregation. The reality of his work was recognized by the national conférence and just before his marriage to Catherine he was given permission to serve as a full-time travelling evangelist.

After two years he was returned to circuit work at Brighouse and then Gateshead. And it was at Gateshead that Catherine preached her first sermon on Whit Sunday 1860. Gateshead proved the nursery for many Salvation Army tactics. Women were given a greater part to play in the services, chapel meetings were advertised with great flamboyance and the problems of poverty were met head-on. On her way to chapel one Sunday evening, she recounted,

I chanced to look up at the thick rows of small windows

above me, where numbers of women were sitting, peering through at the passers-by, or listlessly gossiping with each other. It was suggested to my mind with great power, 'Would you not be doing God more service, and acting more like your redeemer, by turning into some of these houses, speaking to these careless sinners, and inviting them to the service, than by going to enjoy it yourself?' I was startled; it was a new thought . . . I felt greatly agitated and trembled with a sense of my utter weakness, I stood for a moment, looked up to Heaven and said, 'Lord, if Thou wilt help me I will try'; . . . I spoke first to a group of women sitting on a doorstep; and oh, what that effort cost me, words cannot describe! . . . I went on to the next group standing at the entrance to a low dirty court. . . I began to realize that my Master's feet went before me, smoothing my path and preparing my way. This so increased my courage and enkindled my hope, that I ventured to knock at the door of the next house, and when it was opened to go in and speak to the inmates of Jesus . . . I was thinking where I should go next, when I observed a woman standing on an adjoining doorstep, with a jug in her hand. My Divine Teacher said, 'Speak to that woman'. Satan suggested, 'Perhaps she is intoxicated'; but after a momentary struggle I introduced myself to her by saying, 'Are the people out who live on this floor?' observing that the lower part of the house was closed. 'Yes,' she said, 'They are gone to Chapel'. I said, 'Oh, I am so glad to hear that; how is it that you are not going to a place of worship?' 'Me!' she said, looking down upon her forlorn appearance; 'I can't go to chapel; I am kept at home by a drunken husband.' I expressed my sorrow for her and asked if I might come in and see her husband. 'No,' she said, 'he is drunk; you could do nothing with him now.' I replied, 'I do not mind his being drunk, if you will let me come in; I am not afraid' . . . 'Well,' said the woman, 'you can come in if you like but he will only abuse you.' The woman led me to a small room on the first floor, where I found a fine intelligent man, about forty, sitting almost double in a chair, with a jug by his side. . . . As

I began to talk to him, with my heart full of sympathy, he gradually raised himself in his chair and listened with a surprised and half vacant stare. I spoke to him . . . until he was thoroughly waked up, and roused from the stupor in which I found him. His wife wept bitterly and told me that although her husband earned good money, he drank it nearly all and the family were often without food. I read him the parable of the prodigal son, while the tears ran down his face like rain. I then prayed with him . . . I now felt that my work was done.

Salvation Army Farthing Breakfasts in Sunderland in the 1880s.

This was just the beginning of a pattern of visiting which was to become part of everyday Salvation Army work. The need for house-to-house visiting was laid down by William Booth later in his 'Regulations for Officers'.

By hard work and sometimes irregular tactics the Booths quickly raised the Gateshead membership from thirty-nine to three hundred. Congregations grew so rapidly that it was not uncommon for two thousand people to cram into the chapel. Conversions were so numerous the chapel became known as the 'converting shop'.

William was still in demand as a preacher in other places and it was during one of his absences that Catherine took his place. Her reputation as a preacher quickly grew as well, and when the 1861 national conference came to debate the future of this remarkable but unorthodox couple the question of their being given a roving evangelistic role was raised again. When the conference instead decided to appoint them to Newcastle with William only being allowed to spend part of his time away, Catherine, who was watching the proceedings from the gallery, rose in her place and indicated to her husband not to accept. Thus they severed their links with the Methodists.

For the next four years they lived a wandering life leading revivalist campaigns in Cornwall, Cardiff, Walsall, Sheffield and Leeds. During their Cornish campaign it is said that seven thousand people professed conversion. Often Catherine conducted her own independent meetings so that between them they reached the maximum number of people. But still William worried that he was not reaching the outcast poor, although further ingredients of The Salvation Army's methods evolved.

In Walsall, his granddaughter was to recount many years later,

to attract their friends, William announced that 'converted pugilists, horse racers, poachers and others' would speak. 'They say a Hindoo for Hindoos, an African for the Africans, and so a working man for a working men.' It was at Walsall that evening street meetings, preceding the chapel services, were held. I quote from William's diary: 'At night a useful open-air service . . . I was afraid it might fail, I had but few supporters . . . however a crowd gathered . . . I was relying entirely on the inspiration of the moment . . . at the close of an hour and a quarter address during which we sang twice, I invited the people to accompany me to the chapel. Then jumping off the chair, I linked my arm in that of a navvy with a white slop on, and we marched off arm-in-arm'. A crowd followed. This should be remembered as the prototype of The Salvation Army procession.

Despite their growing reputations as evangelists it was a difficult time for the Booths. The family was growing and they frequently had difficulty making ends meet. William and Catherine were often away from each other, and William's letters reflect his gloom at separation and joy when successful conversions could be recounted.

In 1865 the Booth family came to London. One June evening that summer a gospel meeting was being held outside the Blind Beggar public house in London's East End. Those taking part were members of the East London Special Services Committee and the Christian Community. William Booth stopped to listen, but before long he too was preaching. So impressed were the London street evangelists that they invited William to join them and help run a mission in an old tent pitched on a disused Quaker burial ground.

When I saw those masses of poor people [William Booth wrote later], so many of them evidently without God or hope, and found that they so readily and eagerly listened to me, following from open-air meeting to tent, and accepting, in many instances my invitation to kneel at the Saviour's feet there and then, my whole heart went out to them. I walked home and said to my wife: 'Oh Kate, I have found my destiny. These are the people for whose salvation I have been longing all these years. As I passed by the doors of the flaming gin-palaces tonight I seemed to hear a voice sounding in my ears, "Where can you go and find such heathens as these, and where is there so great a need for your labours?" And there and then in my soul I offered up myself and you and the children to this great work. These people shall be our people, and they shall have our God for their God.' And Catherine's response, after some anxious thoughts, 'We have trusted the Lord once for our support and we can trust him again'.

The decision to stay in London brought about an immediate drop in income. As a popular evangelist in Methodist circles William Booth could earn £400 a year. In the East End of London his income was to drop to £3 a week.

The London Booth set out to serve was not the place which served as the capital of a great empire and the lynch-pin of the world monetary system. It was not the place of high society, fashion, great learning and the new scientific ideas. It was the London described by Dickens and later by Jack London and Booth himself. A submerged and extensive slum of human wretchedness. Victorian society was a hierarchy. Booth set out to serve the unfortunates at the bottom of the pile whose only hope of blotting out their misery was drink and yet who were kept hopeless by the drink.

Initially Booth sought to send converts to the existing churches but when they would not go, or the churches did not welcome them, or Booth himself felt he had work for the converts in helping him find new converts, his mind turned to starting his own organization. The result was the founding of a separate agency, The East London Christian Mission. As well as the hostility of the crowds, Booth had the doubts of some of his colleagues to deal with. They were uneasy about the way Booth used the penitent-form, his own device developed from the communion rail to which he could call penitents seeking forgiveness. Booth's emphasis on the doctrine of holiness was questioned, the way he presented the living of an entirely sanctified life to his new converts.

Life for William and Catherine Booth was a constant round of meetings, processions, financial crises, official hostility and public ridicule made bearable by the slow but relentless success of the mission measured in the only way that mattered to them, the winning of souls to God. The Mission soon lost its London tag and became a British agency called simply The Christian Mission. The mission set up stations wherever it went and wherever it could muster sufficient new supporters. As the work grew, William and Catherine came more and more to rely on their son Bramwell and the mission secretary George Scott-Railton.

The mid-Victorian period was an age of religious revival and evangelical preachers. The Christian Mission and the Booths fitted the pattern of the age, but slowly practices evolved within the mission which was to give it its unique durability as The Salvation Army. The power of both Catherine and William as preachers was important. The emphasis on holiness was different. The use of the penitent-form proved very effective as did the use of processions and bands to attract attention. But in addition The Christian Mission stood out as the mission aimed at helping the 'submerged tenth' who would never be seen inside a chapel and whose physical as well as spiritual needs had to be attended to.

Catherine Bramwell-Booth was to write of her grandparents' work in the 1870s in this way:

The Salvation Army had not yet received its name, but in essentials it was formed and fighting. Doctrine and methods exemplified in the work of William and Catherine Booth were, in the main, followed by the 'missioners' paid and voluntary, whom William engaged. Accepted methods included open-air preaching and processioning; the use of secular halls; public testimony of men and women converts; women as well as men preachers; children's meetings in which the children themselves took part; material help of sick and poor; sensational methods to mark events. At funerals, for example, 'Around the house very soon the footpath and streets were blocked with people.'

'. . . A procession followed the hearse to the cemetery, singing hymns all the way . . . Some 2000 people crowded closely round the grave.' Later brass bands led such processions and often sinners knelt in penitence at the grave side. All this, which would be characteristic of The Salvation Army, was building and spreading in The Christian Mission. Unconventional challenging of sinners by Mission members had begun. One started remonstrating with gamblers under a railway arch in Bethnal Green, another opened his shop front and Mission members within shouted the Gospel message in competition with raucous salesmen of the Limehouse Sunday morning market. There was freedom for Mission members—as there still is for Salvation Army officers and soldiers—to attack the devil's strong-holds in any way they thought might be effective.

A further characteristic of the mission which was to become a characteristic of the Army was the system of organization involving a chain of command. The first attempt to give the mission self-government led to the creation of a Methodist-style conference, but this was short-lived. In 1877 conference rule was abolished; William Booth was placed in full and sole command of the Christian Mission and Conference was continued only as a 'Council of war'.

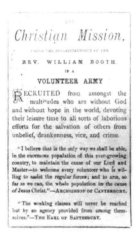

Printer's proof and completed title-page of the Report of the Christian Mission issued in 1878.

Bit by bit military terms crept into the vocabulary of the mission. In 1877 one missioner announced the arrival of the 'Hallelujah Army' to fight the devil in Whitby. He even announced William Booth as the Army's general. In 1878 The Christian Mission Magazine said that the mission had 'organized a salvation army to carry the Blood of Christ and the Fire of the Holy Ghost to every corner of the world'. Early one May morning in 1878 a discussion was taking place in William's bedroom. Bramwell and Railton had been summoned. The preparation of the yearly appeal was in progress. Railton read, 'We are a volunteer army.' Bramwell interrupted with, 'Volunteer! Here, I'm not a volunteer! I'm a regular or nothing!' and William Booth, who was stalking up and down in his dressing-gown, paused, took the pen from Railton's hand, and, stooping over his shoulder, crossed out the word 'volunteer' and wrote 'salvation'.

Spiritually and legally The Salvation Army was established. William Booth was its General and Bramwell Booth his Chief of the Staff. It was but thirteen years since this 'General' had taken his son by the hand and on the doorsteps of that East End gin palace introduced him to 'our people'.

By the end of 1878 the Mission stations had been renamed corps, the first flag was presented and within two or three years the uniform had been generally adopted. The uniform was designed as something plain, distinctive and attractive, a visual testimony in itself to separation from the world.

The War Cry was launched in 1879 and has continued as The Salvation Army's newspaper to this day. The first print-run was 17,000 copies. The front page stories included an account of the acquittal by the magistrates in Boston, Lincolnshire, of a certain Captain Taylor, accused of making too much noise. Captain Cater and his wife in Wednesbury, near Birmingham, describe one of their meetings: 'Glorious time. Three souls saved. Weeping all over the place. The Devil rages. Sinners come out of publics to follow us and get saved. The publicans are crying out. Hallelujah! One sent for me to pray with him, and I believe he is saved!'

'Why a weekly War Cry?' the first editorial asks and then proceeds to answer the question: 'Because The Salvation Army means more war . . .'

And why more war? Because the cry of slaughtered millions rises up louder and louder to heaven, crying to our inmost souls, with irresistible violence, to arise and fight more furiously than ever for the salvation of our fellows from the forces of evil which are dragging them drunken, befouled, degraded, wretched down to an eternity of woe. Because Jesus our King, the dying Jesus of Calvary, still looks weeping on doomed cities and multitudes wandering without a shepherd, and begs us to lay down our lives for them as He laid down his life for us. Because, following in his footsteps, despised, troubled, persecuted, opposed, we have by His continual help tasted victory, seen crowds of captives set at liberty and because we still hear that great voice high above all the noise of many waters bidding us go on to overcome the world.

War! Yes, we will have more war. We will seize on the slain of the daughter of our people; and cleaving to pieces with the sword of truth the wretched victims of unbelief, of drink, of lust, of unfaithful ministry, we will send their quivering parts dripping with a soul's blood into every corner of the world with the cry of 'Woe to him that holdeth back his sword.'

Upon every hill top and from every high tower, shall gleam the blazing signal of war, until the cry of salvation and destruction, for the downfall of Satan's kingdom and for the reign of David's son shall echo and re-echo wherever the English tongue is heard.

No more surrender; no more truce; no more 'masterly inactivity' as to sin and ruin. God will have all men to repent. He will have his own people to repent and do their first works. He will have them abandon for ever all friendship with the world, and all parley with evil hearts. Let all that name the name of Christ depart from iniquity. No more unbelief; no more pride; no more worldly pleasure or worldly dress or show; no more covetousness or self-seeking; no more drinking or smoking or self indulgence of any kind. No more sin! Bought with blood, Israel is to be cleansed with that blood, and to be kept separate and unspotted from the world. Then, and then only, will God restore to Israel that kingdom, that supremacy over all which shall never again pass away. If we will we may be 'the circumcision, which worship God in the Spirit and trust in Jesus Christ, and have no confidence in the flesh'.

Then on to victory! Let every faint heart be strong. No more hanging back to let others fight. No more keeping religion to yourself, or doing good in a quiet way, while the smoke of tormented millions rises blacker and blacker up from the eternal pit of woe, and the wail of anguish bursts from dying lips, from dying souls on every side, and the dance of sin and death goes madly on over the very corpses of the mutilated slain. To every lip the trumpet, and from every heart the life and death cry of warning and hope! Above all the din of the world's rattle, above the storms of bitter enmity to Christ, above the roar of every tempest of woe that bursts upon a sin-bound world let the King's name be heard, loud and clear, till not by tens or thousands merely, but by millions, those who have hated and refused Him fall weeping at His feet, to take up the easy yoke, and then to rise and swell the lines of victory. Salvation, always, everywhere!

With The Salvation Army finding its name and founding its newspaper, with members donning uniforms and taking ranks, the Army had found both its style and doctrine. It was a mainstream evangelical Christian body with certain unorthodox methods and certain unusual emphases of doctrine.

Winning souls was to be the supreme goal of the Army, with converts being encouraged to lead holy lives and dedicate themselves to converting others. One condition of becoming a soldier in the Army, however, was that the taking of all intoxicating drink had to be forsworn. Catherine Booth wrote a pamphlet on the subject:

We have no hesitation in affirming that strong drink is Satan's chief instrument for keeping the masses of many countries under his power. What is to be done? How shall we deal with the drink? We answer in the name of Christ and humanity—deal with it as with all other Satan-invented, Christ-dishonouring, soul-ruining abominations. Wash your hands of it at once and for ever, and give a united and straightforward testimony to the world that you consider it an enemy of all righteousness and the legitimate offspring of Satan.

I submit that there is no other way for Christians to deal with strong drink. All other ways have been tried and have failed. The time has come for Christians to denounce the use of intoxicating drinks as irreligious and immoral.

With the help of its unwavering rule on drink many thousands of alcoholics have been able to give up drinking and return to normal life.

William Booth was also convinced that wearing black and indulging in the excesses of mourning was opposed to the teaching of Christ. He introduced a cross and crown badge to be worn by Salvationists as a sign of bereavement and encouraged funerals to be turned into occasions for evangelism.

While for many years The Christian Mission baptized infants and administered the Lord's supper monthly, William Booth gradually came to the view that the sacraments were merely symbols of spiritual truth. He sought after the experience which the symbols represented. Children are now not baptized in the Army but dedicated. Converts are accepted as soldiers at a special ceremony where they publicly confess their faith.

William Booth called upon his soldiers to realize that their spiritual life was dependent upon a continuous recognition of their union with Christ as their Saviour and the supplier of every need. And at every meal he would have them remember that Christ's body was broken for their salvation. He encouraged faith in the possibility of holy living. When the Army was born, John Wesley, the great revivalist and holiness preacher of the eighteenth century through whose writings the general himself was led into the experience of holiness, had been dead over seventy years. Many of his followers were beginning to neglect his teaching concerning holy living. The Salvation Army hoisted anew the banner of holiness, and holiness meetings became from the first a regular feature of Salvation Army activity.

From its very earliest days the Army embraced a spirit of internationalism. First moves were to the British Empire and the English-speaking world. Continental Europe followed. In 1879 a soldier from the Coventry corps emigrated to Philadelphia in the United States. The first open-air meeting was held by the soldier, Amos Shirley, at the junction of Fourth and Oxford Streets. Early work was promising and Commissioner George Scott-Railton with seven others was despatched across the Atlantic to help. By May 1880 Booth was cabled the news that the Army had sixteen officers, forty cadets and over four hundred soldiers. In the spring of 1880 the Army was also on the advance in Australia. A call went out from a mission meeting in Adelaide for General Booth to send an officer. In January 1881 the first captain set sail.

About the same time an advance party of Salvationists set sail for France. With them was Florence Soper, a doctor's daughter, whose father was none too pleased with her dalliance with the Army. But Florence was a determined young lady.

What strange experiences in that gay city [she wrote of Paris]. Cox and I made sandwich boards and walked up and down the boulevards causing immense astonishment . . . soon our hall was filled every night.

The disorder in the meetings increased. When we started singing, the crowd of hooligans—we had very few women in the meetings—would use their own words, laughing uproariously. The song for the prayer-meeting with the chorus 'approchez-vous' was turned by them into 'embrassez-vous'.

A young lieutenant from England was sent to help us keep order. His hair was red and caused much fun, our roughs pretending to light their cigars by it. He was terribly knocked about by them, but had wonderful patience and I think never lost his temper.

Florence Soper was to become Mrs Bramwell Booth. First, however, she became a Salvation Army officer and when in October 1882 she and Bramwell married she wore her Army uniform. Dr Soper found it difficult to approve an 'Army' wedding for his daughter but was present to see the brass band lead the couple in procession to the hall.

'God is more than good to me,' wrote Bramwell of his marriage. 'I feel I have found a rock,' wrote Florence, 'and I only want now to learn how to help him.'

The general wrote to them in Southborough, during their honeymoon, long letters of Army news. He was 'more glad than I can say' to know they were happy but keen to get his Chief of Staff back in the office. Army work always called.

2

'Bootheration'

When Catherine, first child of Bramwell and Florence Booth, was born in July 1883 The Salvation Army was only five years old. She was born in the midst of the most crucial and vital years of the Army's development, those twelve years from 1878, when the Army found its name, to 1890, the year of the death of baby Catherine's grandmother Catherine, wife of the Army's founder and general.

They were years of growth and turmoil. They were the years in which the whole idea of donning a uniform to proclaim the Christian gospel in the streets was so revolutionary that it attracted ridicule and hostility. The Army was mocked by the comfortable classes, physically attacked by the street roughs and harassed by the law.

Today the Army is such an established institution and its uniformed officers, soldiers and brass bands so familiar a sight that it is hard to imagine the time when it was the butt of offensive jokes in *Punch* and the object of scorn of the middle classes.

In the month of Catherine's birth, *Punch* had this to say about the Army's processions. Under the heading 'Bootheration' Mr Punch wrote:

A Procession is a nuisance at any time, and should only be permitted on rare and exceptional occasions. As to the noisy Religious Services which disturb the peace and quiet of neighbourhoods on the Day of Rest, they should all be confined within the four walls of their own Tabernacle, Camp, Church, or Conventicle, whatever it may be, and those walls should be, by Act of Parliament, of a sufficient thickness to prevent the escape of noise. . . .

If the maxim of 'Keep yourselves to yourselves, and don't say nothing to nobody,' were accepted upon by all these so-called, or self-styled, Religious Bodies, how much happier we should all be. 'Inquirers after Truth' can call on them, and if they find Truth at home . . . they can step inside and remain there. Only don't let the different parties parade the streets, and come out and disturb good folks who, unable to forego their absolutely necessary work even on Sunday, are compelled to remain at home and to find their religious service in the practical maxim *Laborare est orare*; or those more fortunate who would make holiday of rest in the open air, away from the Screechers, the Preachers, the Ranters, and Canters. An Englishman's home is his castle,—if it is a public-house it may be his Elephant and Castle,—and an Englishman's House of Prayer should be as private as his Castle; but, even in his own house, if an Englishman is a nuisance to his neighbour, the 'aggrieved parishioner' has his remedy. Liberty for all, but don't make too free with Liberty.

The prejudiced and pontificating Mr Punch had singularly failed to appreciate the fact that in the Victorian London of his day there were many English men and women who were homeless and who lived on the streets and it was these people, neglected for so long by the society in which they existed, who were to be the target of the Army's work.

Objections to the noise of street parades and outdoor meetings were the tip of an iceberg of disquiet. The respectable classes knew that the activities of the Army threatened to undermine a system of hypocrisy and sectional interest so successfully masked by the outward trappings of Victorian prudery. The brewers and publicans saw the works of the Army as a direct challenge to their lucrative way of life. The conservative elements of both church and government establishment viewed the successes of the Army as an unsettling challenge to the existing order and to their authority.

In the eyes of so many vested interests the Army's chief crime was its very success. For every Christian Mission

*The Chief of Staff and Mrs Bramwell Booth with their daughters
(l. to r.) Mary, Catherine and Miriam in 1890.*

station in Britain in 1878, by 1886 there were twenty Salvation Army corps. For every evangelist in 1878, by 1886 there were twenty-five commissioned officers. In the financial year 1877–8 the Mission spent £4,362. In the financial year 1884–5 the balance sheet of the Army shows an expenditure of nearly £76,000.

When hostile mobs, backed and no doubt fortified by the publicans, began to attack the Salvationists the police often turned a blind eye. If arrests were made it was the Salvationists who were dealt with more severely than their attackers. Shortly before Catherine's birth, in one twelve-month period, 669 Salvationists were assaulted. Fifty-six Army buildings were stormed and damaged and eighty-six members of the Army were jailed by the magistrates. The mobs, often organized into what they called a 'Skeleton Army', had great sport at the Salvationists' expense.

The General and his troops fought on and many deeds of individual heroism have gone down in the Army's annals. At seaside Hastings, the Army's first martyr received fatal injuries from a barrage of rocks and putrid fish. She was kicked and left to die in a back alley. At Folkestone in Kent a local clergyman offered a cash prize to the first rough to capture the Army standard, 'a bastard flag that represents nothing and nobody'.

At Worthing, another English south-coast resort, local boarding-house keepers complained that the activities of the Army had ruined one of the town's finest seasons. *The Worthing Gazette* described the Salvationists as 'excitable young men and hysterical young women who mistake a quasi-religious revelry for godliness'. The Worthing Skeleton Army had every backing. Even the Chief Constable wrote that the Skeletons received 'considerable encouragement from those in a higher social position'.

One August Sunday afternoon in 1884 the matter came to a head. The intrepid Captain Ada Smith, aged only twenty-three, took her band and procession of Salvationists onto the streets. After enduring an hour of abuse from the Skeleton Army with the police standing by, the small contingent of Salvationists was set upon by the roughs. They managed to escape from the scrummage that ensued into the hall they rented. But the safety of the hall was short-lived. The next evening as the Salvationists were at prayer the mob attacked again, this time hurling missiles at the hall and smashing the windows.

The situation went from bad to worse. When The Salvation Army's landlord was attacked in his shop he fired his revolver at the intruders. Two of the Skeletons were injured. When the first of the Skeletons was brought to justice such disorder arose in the town that the Riot Act had to be read. By this device the authorities had the powers to clear the streets. A running battle resulted between the cavalry and the Skeleton Army. An armed police guard was placed outside the Salvationists' citadel.

On the third Sunday after the first major head-on clash the Skeletons invaded the afternoon service. The police followed and a pitched battle was fought where only minutes before an act of worship had been in progress. The scenes of mayhem and havoc spread outside. The whole bloody event came to a sudden end when the Skeletons again attacked the shop owned by the landlord of the Salvationists' hall. The Skeleton Army fled in disarray as George Head fired his gun again and again to protect his shop and himself. He was later found by a jury not guilty of maliciously wounding one of the Skeleton Army leaders.

As the young Catherine learned to walk and talk in the security of her parents' home, The Salvation Army was still at the stage in its development when physical assault on soldiers was commonplace. Despite her vivid memories of her father returning home bloodied after an attack and her memories of the roughs who came to the family's local corps at Barnet, her chief recollection of childhood is the loving family unit.

'When I was eighteen months old, or perhaps two years, I was sitting in a high chair by the piano. My mother was playing the piano. Although she couldn't sing—she wasn't musical like my father—she was singing in her style the chorus, "We'll cross the River of Jordan, Happy, Happy". And then, my mother remembered, the baby clapped her hands and said, " 'appy, 'appy", and that was my first army chorus, "Happy in the Lord". There were seven of us, quite a family today. We were all musical and we sang together. I should think we sang very acceptably; at any rate, we sang for our own pleasure. We found some peculiar old songs in the songbook. For instance there was one which I don't think is used now, "Where is now the good Elijah?" I can still remember how the tune went, and we used to sing it with such fervour. We would put in other names, "Where is now the good Daniel?"—all bible characters. "Safely in the promised land" was the coming together at the end. It was a style that was very good for children, free and easy yet sincere. They all had a message for us. I

General Booth's visit to Hitchin in 1908.

think they helped us. They helped me, I know, to believe that God was real and that Jesus's death on the cross really happened. Jesus and the cross can make an impression upon children, very young children, that isn't realized today. My mother believed that we couldn't be too young to begin to know and to begin to be familiar with the story of Christianity.

'However, I reckon it has been one of the difficulties of my life that I never had a great moment of conversion. I sometimes used to feel: oh, I wish I'd been a great sinner and could see a great difference between my life before and my life after. But I was four years old or thereabouts when I gave myself to Christ.

'I had been naughty. I had grieved my mother. I don't now know what it was but I had been naughty. My mother was praying with me, and she prayed with me that the Lord Jesus would forgive me. I don't remember exactly what she said; I wish I could. Then she said to me, "Now, Cath, you pray, darling; tell Jesus you want to be good." Well, I prayed and did as she said—I promised, I spoke as I felt without stopping to consider each word. It's a wonderful thing, you see, children don't stop to think about faith, or how can God hear me? Such a thought never entered my head. I prayed and gave myself to Christ. That, I think, was my first step. Oh, I've often wished that I could have had a more definite step. Of course I have taken steps forward since then. When I was fourteen or so, I had an experience that helped me further on. But otherwise life has been trusting God, obeying what I am prompted to do by his Holy Spirit, and it is up to God to do the rest.'

The story of Catherine's father's conversion makes an interesting comparison. Bramwell was seven years old when his father went to Cardiff to conduct a mission in a circus tent. Many years later Catherine recounted the story in the biography of her father which she wrote in the 1930s.

Whilst at Cardiff his parents held a series of meetings in a circus. These the child attended; they made him unhappy. One sees him there, his sensitive face set in lines of defence, his little head held high. He was the preacher's son and proud even if he were unhappy too! Then one evening during the after-meeting his mother came and sat beside him. Their eyes met. No one who noticed Bramwell Booth ever failed to notice his eyes, brown, luminous, steadfast, his mother's eyes over again people said. What a picture, these two, amongst the heterogeneous crowd, so like each other; so close in love to each other; the small creature whom it had been his mother's aim to train in that 'implicit, uncompromising obedience,' lifting his eyes to hers, and, in answer to her invitation to give himself to Christ, saying deliberately, 'No!' This is how he tells of it:

'She said to me with great tenderness, "you are very unhappy." When I replied, "Yes," she added, "You know the reason," and again I had to say "Yes." Then came the clear question as to giving myself to God and I said "No." She put her hands suddenly to her face, and I can never forget my feeling on seeing the tears fall through them on to the sawdust beneath her feet. I knew what those tears represented. But still I said "No."

She says: 'For some little time I had been anxious on his behalf. He had appeared deeply convicted during the services, and one night at the circus I had urged him very earnestly to decide for Christ. For a long time he could not speak, but I insisted on his giving me a definite answer as to whether he would accept the offer of salvation or not. I shall never forget the feeling that thrilled through my soul when my darling boy, only seven years old, about whom I had formed such high expectations with regard to his future service to the Master, deliberately looked me in the face and answered, "No".'

He continued, he tells us, in this unhappy frame of mind: 'Sin was revealed in me and I came to see how its power was slowly increasing. My parents treated me with loving patience. They did not say much to me except when alone, and then led my thoughts rather away from myself. I remember however, how my father's prayers at family worship seemed to take on a new meaning for me.'

The strong sense of guilt which pressed so heavily upon the child's heart was not occasioned by flagrant naughtiness. People thought him a remarkably good child. His affectionate disposition protected him from selfishness and bad temper. He did not know the meaning of jealousy. His mother says he never told a lie, nor did his conduct ever cause her five minutes' real anxiety. Yet there is no doubt he was vividly conscious of wrong. He did not want to be religious, above all he wanted his own way, in spite of his mother—in spite of God.

About three months after that 'No' in Cardiff, they went to Walsall, where an eight weeks' Mission was conducted. Attending some of the meetings the child's misery became more acute. He says: 'I felt myself in a new and more serious way to be a sinner'. He gave up his games; began to pray in a kind of fervour of fear for help, but in spite of all, 'I could not bring myself to say "Yes", where I had already said "No".' Nevertheless the moment came. His mother held some meetings for children only, and in one of those the boy made his decision. He does not remember anything of what was said, possibly he was not influenced by any word spoken then. He must, as we know, have gone to the meeting with his little heart in a turmoil of rebellious unhappiness. Whether what his mother actually said on that occasion helped him is immaterial; some influence moved him, his resistance was broken, his will yielded.

His mother did not see him stand up and take the step, but 'discovered' him, as she says, when writing of it to her mother, 'at the communion rail among a crowd of little penitents. He had come out of his own accord from the middle of the hall, and I found him squeezed in among the rest, confessing his sin.' Here he kneels, as he himself describes it, 'ashamed and broken up'.

A young man, of whom nothing is known, spoke to him. Whoever he was, it is evident he had a clear notion of the importance of what he was doing. He does not seem to have had any idea who the child was, but had he been vouchsafed a vision of what the little penitent would live to accomplish this unknown servant of Christ could hardly have added to the zeal and wisdom with which he dealt with the boy. All his life Bramwell Booth remembered with gratitude and appreciation the thoroughness and spiritual insight of this unknown disciple of Christ. The moment was even more critical than could have been understood by those who shared it. Anyone knowing the child's affectionate and sensitive nature might well have thought to help the little fellow's distress by comforting words about God's love, but, led of the Spirit, far from playing the part of comforter, this unknown man made the child's already burdened heart ready to break from shame and fear. He called for a confession of the sins for which forgiveness was being sought. Speaking of it years afterwards, Bramwell Booth said:

'He made me confess my wickedness, made me realize what a fearful thing it was to want my own way—it was going against the One who died for us. I saw that it was. And that pride was the sin that sank Satan into hell. He said, "it will send you there too," and I felt it would.'

So he led the child down the steep way of humiliation and self-abhorrence which souls of no matter what age must all tread if their quest is to end in the discovery that Christ 'hath power to forgive sin'. In his distress the child cried aloud, and then his unknown interlocuter left him. A little later his mother knelt beside him, put her hand lovingly upon his head, prayed with him, 'and led me to cast myself with faith in His promise upon my Saviour. Gradually light came to me, and the accusing sense of guilt was taken away, and then my Lord gave the assurance that I was forgiven and made one of his own.' Thus he writes of it. Thus was the first spiritual conflict ended. Many were to follow, but the certainty of this victory, with the accompanying reality of the preceding confusion and rebellion, of the sense of helplessness and guilt, of the ensuing sense of peace and release, was never dimmed.

Throughout his formative years, the young Bramwell's parents lived a restless, itinerant life. By contrast Catherine's home life was stable. Despite the Army's trials which impinged themselves on family life, Catherine and her six siblings were brought up in what was essentially a Victorian middle-class household, in the North London suburb of Hadley Wood, near Barnet.

'How different London was in the eighties and nineties. To begin with it was full of horses. And what we suffered as children seeing the overloaded horses. Many a time at home we would see a horse struggling up Mosely Hill with a cart of swedes and then, if we could, we would persuade the driver to let us empty half the load and we promised that we would run with them. We picked up the swedes and ran to the top of the hill to put them back on the cart. And I still feel the horror of seeing a horse lying on its side in a London street with a man perhaps sitting on its head. It was an awful anxiety. Even now I mustn't remember it at night or I shouldn't sleep.

'But what a joy to be on the top of a bus—they had no roofs then—and sit in the front next to the driver and talk

Florence Booth in the schoolroom with (l. to r.) Catherine, Miriam, Bernard, Olive and Mary. On the table is the current issue of The War Cry, *March 4th 1899.*

to him about the horses. Oh, what your excitements were in those days! And I remember the muffin man balancing his green baize top on his head and ringing his bell and then you ran out of the house and brought crumpets or muffins according to your taste. I liked those.

'None of us went to school, neither the boys nor the girls. My mother educated me. The younger girls had a governess because an old great-aunt, when she died, left her little bit all to my mother. It was almost nothing, £80 a year or something like that. She was a darling old lady. She lived with my grandfather on the Soper side. He made a home for her. She hadn't much money, just a little. But my mother's joy in spending that money! I can remember the feeling that we were so rich.

'At any rate, one of the things my mother did with the money was to pay for a governess. You could get a good governess in those days for much less than you could get one today. So the younger girls had a governess who came once or twice a week.

'We had at that time an Irish terrier, a red-haired terrier; it was a most awful fighter. He fought all the dogs in the district. One day the governess was seriously lecturing the children on some subject and they were all sitting there like angels when the sound of a dog-fight drifted through the air and before she had time to look around the classroom was empty. All the children had jumped out the window and flown up the garden path to see where the fight was.

'I distinctly remember the lessons with my mother. We had a schoolroom in the house. She came in at nine o'clock. We were supposed by then to have cleared everything and we sat there two of us on each side. She came in to take the lesson, whatever it might be, and she was a wonderful teacher. She made us enjoy all the subjects, even arithmetic, which I was very weak on. She was keen on mental arithmetic. She used to give us sums on the spot. She taught us the rudiments of algebra. She also taught us German from Otto's Grammar. We had a French maid always so we got a good grounding in practical French. Above all I would put that she taught me to love reading. By the time I was in my teens I had learned how to have a book that was mine and to be friends with that book.

'She also read aloud to us. She had a most beautiful reading voice. We used to lie either on our backs or face down, on the floor, because it was good for our spines, and then Mama read aloud. I think she read all Dickens, Trollope, Thackeray and heaps of others I could mention. I first came to know them by listening to my mother's voice. Very precious. Then when you came to read the book for yourself you very often made a friend of the book. At least I did.

'I can still hear my mother's voice reading. She familiarized us with all the standard works, which many people don't bother to read now. But they were very wonderful books. All the Brontës of course, George Eliot and I think all the main writers of the day were made our friends by her.

'We were allowed to read *The Times*, which came into the house, and generally another one of the picture papers, *The Graphic* or something. But I don't remember discussing the issues of the day. Of course The Salvation Army used to have as one of its main tenets—no politics. It's in the regulations that you may not let any Army hall for a political meeting.

'What I do remember is having a tremendous interest in the Boer War. The Army began its work amongst soldiers and sailors at that time. Miss Murray, I think her father was a general, who became Colonel Murray in The Salvation Army, was the first in charge of that work. She went to South Africa to establish things—tea places and rest places for the troops. And we, with Mama, paid for three dozen copies of *The War Cry* and we had the addresses of three dozen Salvationists who were out there fighting. Of course we were on the British side, we wanted to beat the Boers all right. We enjoyed it, we got very excited about it. We had the news and we addressed these three dozen copies of *The War Cry* to individual Salvationists and had letters from some of them. And then we went down to the local post pillar-box, put them in and said "God bless you" to each one. "God bless you, God bless you." What we thought that would do I don't know, but we did it. We heard the news of all the events, the Relief of Mafeking. We were tremendously interested in what the Army was doing.

'When I was a girl we had a full household of people working in the house. We had a nursemaid, housemaid, kitchenmaid, cook, and for a long time later we had someone who answered the phone. The phone in our house, when my father was there, was very important. We got a

phone as soon as we could as it was a business. It kept my
father in touch with headquarters. To begin with we had
no such thing, no telephone, no electricity, no petrol, no
cars—you can't compare life then with life now in any way.
The phone is pretty bad now. We are always being
interrupted. Meals interrupted: phone! Somebody has to

Florence Booth and slum children at a turn-of-the-century Christmas.

rush to answer it. Still, what a comfort and what a strange
world it would be now to me without it.

'We had a tremendous wealth of happiness out of our
pets: guinea pigs, rats, a canary at one time, but not for
long as we didn't fancy keeping a bird in a cage. We were
always learning about birds and watching birds with our
binoculars. Mice were my great favourites as pets. And as

children we were so excited about the tadpoles turning into little frogs, growing their legs. And the toad that was tame marching so carefully. Life is so full of interesting things. Even toads, wonderful creatures. I constantly thank God for letting me grow up in the country, what we should call the country now, the fields. I think how dreadful it is that the town child misses so much. There's a great difference if you've only got pavements. You can't run barefoot on the pavements. They are so filthy. Whereas we could run barefoot in the fields until our feet got quite hardened. It was clean, so different.

'I learned to play in the corps band at Barnet. I had a tenor horn and it felt wonderful. It was a wonderful feeling marching with the little band of ten or twelve. Then I was promoted to second cornet and then to first cornet. I became more and more important as a bandswoman.

'People were aware that I was the granddaughter of the General and it was a bit of a torment. People always seemed to expect us to be able to do things simply because Booth was our name. I used to feel so unequal to it. I often used to pray in those days, "Lord help me. I can love thee and love sinners more, but that's all I can do. The others are better at talking and singing solo." There it was, a problem we had to face.

'I wanted to be good. I wanted to please my parents. I don't think I was consciously disobedient, but I was condemned to doubt. I questioned so much. That was my agony.

'I had got an unbelieving heart. God has been very patient with me. I talked freely with my parents, especially my mother, but I never told them that I was really tempted to doubt the whole thing. It would have broken their hearts, you see. I knew they were so set upon our being good. I talked with my sisters. They all looked to me to be their guide. They used to come and tell me things. I remember having a talk with my sister Miriam. She said, "Oh, I feel so wrong because I doubt." I thought to myself that I had had to come through my own doubts to understand what she was feeling. They all came to me in one way or another and that compelled me to settle the question for myself.

'In my life I have had so many times of doubt. You have to settle it, to fight it out for yourself. Then you come through the darkness, as I call it, the questioning. Some things you will never understand; you simply have to leave them with God and go on, go on trusting.

'We were a close family. We sang together and kept Christmas and birthdays. They were all-important to us.

'Although we lived in a comfortable house, we weren't remote from the people the Army was there to help. When I lived at home, before I became an officer, we all walked two miles from home to the Barnet Corps, to which we belonged. Our interests were there and I visited the sick and the homes of drunkards when I was little more than a child of twelve or thirteen. I didn't understand what it was all about, but I began to understand and I began to hate the drink with a proper Salvation Army hatred. I don't remember the first time I went into a public house—I dare say I should—but it was in Barnet. The Green Man was the worst public house, the biggest public house in Barnet in those days and our soldiers used to go there. I went with them as a child—but I was never abused or ill-treated.

'We were all soldiers at Barnet. We became soldiers at the age of twelve. We felt very important. I learned there the sorrow of the drink, the terrible curse it was. I was very much interested in a small boy who came to what was then the Band of Love, of which I had charge. I was twelve or fourteen at the time. He fell ill and I went to see him. He was all blown up with dropsy. And the landlady where he and his father lived said, "You know, sister, it's his father's drinking that made the boy sick like he is." That was my first face-to-face encounter with the anguish of families where there is a drunkard.

'We got accustomed to the idea that the Army was ridiculed and shouted at at the corps where we went as children. It was common everywhere. And I can't help thinking that it established a certain relationship with the ruffians in the town. They and the Army were friends, and they played a very important part in our meetings. They used to make up parodies of the songs, the choruses we used to sing. "Over Jordan" was one. "We shall rest our weary feet by the crystal waters sweet", we sang, describing heaven. Then the roughs used to shout, "Over Jordan we shall wash our dirty feet." Yells from the gallery: "We shall wash our dirty feet in the Jordan waters sweet." We learnt to care about the people, and of course that is what The Salvation Army is supposed to be doing everywhere. That is the reason there is an Army. My father said, "If anyone asks you 'What's The Salvation Army?' you should say, 'The Salvation Army is love for souls, caring about helping the people to be good'." And the Army is also about believing the children. William Booth was converted when he was fifteen. What a difference in the world if every boy of fifteen got converted!

'We were aware from my very earliest stage about the need for money. Money came into my prayers. "Oh Lord, send money so that Papa won't be so worried." They were frightfully short of money. Sometimes they hadn't the money to get the letters away.'

When Catherine was only two years old an event took place which proved the turning-point in the Army's history. Bramwell Booth appeared in the dock at the Old Bailey charged with abducting a young girl. In his history of The Salvation Army, *No Discharge in This War*, General Frederick Coutts told the story in this way:

The four of them [Bramwell Booth, William Stead of the *Pall Mall Gazette*, Mrs Josephine Butler, campaigning wife of an Anglican clergyman, and Benjamin Scott, Chamberlain of the City of London] determined to make their own private investigations into the presence of young children in brothels. Between them they guaranteed the sum of two hundred pounds for expenses and their eventual plan was that a child of obvious innocence and under the legal age should be procured for an agreed sum in order to demonstrate with what ease those who were no more than children could be secured to stock the country's brothels. Only by some drastic action could public opinion be aroused and an unwilling House of Commons be compelled to act.

Mrs Butler suggested that Rebecca Jarrett, who she

and her husband had taken under their wing would be the one to find a suitable girl. She was a former procuress, at the time in her late thirties, who had been seduced at the age of twelve. This was not so important as it might sound for, with the help of Mrs Butler, Rebecca had set up a tiny home in Winchester where she cared for girls in moral need. But though Rebecca did not hide from Stead the kind of woman she had been, she begged to be excused from returning, even for a day, and for an innocent purpose, to her old role. In carrying out his wishes she would not be able to avoid a measure of deceit and lying. But Stead would not be denied. He would expose the evil trade in the columns of the Gazette. None would escape the day of his anger. In his attitude to Rebecca he was—to use his own word—'inexorable'. With tears Rebecca finally consented. Stead could hardly have imagined that his carefully planned precautions to advise in advance such public figures as (amongst others) the Archbishop of Canterbury and Cardinal Manning of his plans would be of no avail in the day of his trial. How much less poor Rebecca who knew only too well, from her own hard life, of the hazards of such an experiment. But after several false starts she found and paid for a child named Eliza Armstrong whose mother was far too casual and drunken. Perhaps the fatal mistake was that though Rebecca could testify that Mrs Armstrong had agreed to part with the child, Eliza, she had not secured similar word from the child's reputed Father.

Eliza was then taken to an agreed address which Stead himself visited while she was there, after which a trusted woman officer took the girl to a specialist who certified that she was virgo intacta. Stead then changed his mind about the girl being sent down to Winchester with Rebecca, and said that she had better leave the country in order to be out of reach of her mother. But by now Eliza would not go with anyone save Rebecca, so Bramwell Booth arranged for both of them to cross to France in the care of Madame Combe, a soldier of the Geneva corps. On Monday July 6th, 1885, the first of

Stead's articles appeared under the title of 'The Maiden Tribute of Modern Babylon', and these continued daily until the tenth.

The run on the Pall Mall Gazette defied description. Police had to be sent to clear Northumberland Avenue. Newsboys hawked single copies at Ludgate Circus for half-a-crown apiece. Finding that station bookstalls were refusing to handle the Gazette, William Booth opened headquarters as a distribution centre. George Bernard Shaw offered to take as many copies as he could carry and peddle them in the streets. When the City of London solicitor had a score or more newsboys arrested for selling obscene matter, a group of unemployed costermongers besieged the Gazette offices eager to defeat any attempt to suppress the paper by selling it themselves.

With much that Stead wrote the Army was not directly involved, for he did not limit himself to the simple story of Eliza Armstrong. He gave the entire trade the full treatment—the padded rooms in the West End establishments, the decoying of country girls to town, the bribes paid out by the organizers of the traffic, and the corruption of those who, for their own gain, turned a blind eye to its iniquities. If much of the Victorian dirt had been swept under the carpet, Stead swept it out into the face of the public. Opinion was either hotly for him or violently against him. The Times described his campaign as an 'intemperate and discreditable agitation' which 'blackened the name of England before the world'. But a Saturday afternoon rally gathered a quarter of a million supporters around a banner inscribed 'Honour to the Pall Mall Gazette'.

Within seventeen days a petition carrying three hundred and ninety-thousand signatures was carried by eight Salvation Army cadets into the House of Commons and laid on the floor beside the mace because there was no table large enough to hold it, praying that:

'the age of consent be raised to eighteen;

'the procuring of young people for immoral purposes be made a criminal offence;

'a magistrate be given power to issue an order for entry

into any house where it is believed that girls are being
detained against their will;

'as it is now a criminal act for a woman to solicit a
man, it be made equally criminal for a man to solicit a
woman.'

On August 14th the Criminal Law Amendment Act,
reckoned before Whitsuntide to be stone dead, was
revived and carried by one hundred and seventy-nine
votes to seventy-one with the age of consent raised to
sixteen. A thanksgiving meeting was held in the Exeter
Hall.

But the sting was in the tail of the story. Mrs
Armstrong began to worry about Eliza. Where was she?
When would she be back? She tried to get in touch with
Rebecca Jarrett. Her supposed concern was noted by a
reporter from Lloyd's Newspaper, a rival of the Pall Mall
Gazette. Mrs Armstrong, casting herself in the role of a
distraught mother, asked a magistrate at the Marylebone
police court what she ought to do. The police were told
to make some enquiries. The reporter kept his nose to
the scent. Lloyd's splashed the story of the missing Eliza,
the efforts of her mother to find her, the crowded street
that hailed the girl's return. A question was asked in
the House. The Home Secretary replied that he was
consulting the Attorney General. On September 8th
Stead, Bramwell Booth, Rebecca Jarrett and three others
were charged with unlawfully taking away Eliza
Armstrong from the custody of her parents and of inde-
cently assaulting the aforesaid Eliza. Passions now boiled
over. The defendants were attacked outside the Bow
Street police court and hissed inside it. The police begged
Bramwell Booth not to appear in his Salvation Army
uniform because of the hostility it provoked. The Black
Maria proved a haven of refuge from the rough handling
of the crowd. In committing the accused for trial at the
Old Bailey the Bow Street magistrate said that their
action had 'greatly lowered the English people in the
estimation of foreign lands'.

At the Old Bailey hearing which opened on October
23rd a single major ruling by Mr Justice Lopes virtually

determined the course of events. He supported the judgement of the lower court that any evidence as to the
motives which had governed Stead's actions were inad-
missible. So the Archbishop of Canterbury waited in
vain to speak. It was enough for the judge that Eliza
Armstrong had been taken away without her father's
consent, and consent gained by fraud was no consent at
all. When the jury, in considering their verdict, wished
to distinguish between abduction for criminal purposes
and the technical offence which Stead and Rebecca
Jarrett had committed, Mr Lopes repeated that no
motive, however high-minded, justified the taking away
of a child from her parents without their consent. With
the case narrowed down to this one point, the acquittal
of Bramwell Booth was virtually assured but the fate of
Stead and the others was sealed. The truth was that
neither Stead nor Rebecca Jarrett need have been
convicted, for the records at Somerset House later
revealed that Charles Armstrong was not Eliza's father;
she was an illegitimate child.

So a verdict of guilty was returned and sentences were
passed under the Act of 1861 under which many a
procurer in London could have been charged, but never
was! Stead was given three months which he served in
the first division. Rebecca was given six months but
without hard labour. In court she was torn between her
loyalties to her old companions, to whom she had turned
in order to help Stead to secure Eliza, and her new
friends. Her evidence was confused and at times contrad-
ictory, lest her former confederates should scorn
her—who now claimed to be leading a new and better
life—for breaking her word to them. But when she came
out of prison she was met by Mrs Bramwell Booth and,
under another name, lived for forty years as a faithful
Salvationist. Eliza was cared for as well, and later
married happily.

If it had been feared that such a court case involving the
son of the general would be a scandal to ruin the reputation
of the Army, the result was almost the opposite. The Army

was seen to be at the very centre of the battle it claimed to be waging and in the public's eyes its standing increased as its courage was witnessed.

What part did the young toddler Catherine play in this high drama? It was her baby sister who was taken to court by her mother as she was still being nursed. Without realizing it Catherine could have played quite an important role.

For Rebecca Jarrett the road leading her away from her old life was long and hard. It started in 1884 in Northampton. She entered the care of The Salvation Army after collapsing at a meeting. There followed a painful period of rehabilitation and conversion and at one point Rebecca almost gave up.

'My mother tells me that she was having quite a struggle with Rebecca, who said, "It's no good, Mrs Booth, I'm going"; and my mother said after she had talked and prayed to no avail, "Before you go, will you have a cup of tea, Rebecca? Hold the baby for me." And she pushed me into the woman's arms, certain that she wouldn't run away if my mother left the room because she had got the baby to hold. So, I reckon, I was pushed into service fairly early in life.'

If Rebecca had left there would have been no trial and no arousal of public opinion against one of the worst and most hypocritical evils of the day. Young Catherine might not have been aware of her important role at the time but she does have one memory of the events of 1885.

'I remember the Black Maria calling and my father coming home bleeding, having been pelted with stones. He didn't really explain to me what was happening. I just knew. God never explains anything to us. God gives his commands in The Salvation Army.

'But when we were young we were sheltered in many ways from the real conditions of life in London. We lived in a newly developed estate so that we weren't living in town. We didn't see the seamy side of life until we went into the pubs in Barnet and I prayed for people that I knew were drunkards and didn't always win them.

'I was nineteen when I left home, and I thought I had

parted with everything that made life precious to me: the younger children, whom I loved devotedly (I was the eldest of the seven), my parents, whom I loved to distraction, you might almost say. They were both in their way perfect people. The whole life had to be sacrificed, and I went to live among strangers in the officer training college and then to be appointed to my first post.'

3

In Darkest England

At the time of Catherine's birth, her grandfather was a
well-known figure. Some saw him as a figure of fun, others
viewed him as a dangerous radical, and in ecclesiastical
circles he was often suspected of being a zealot. Physically
he was impressive. Tall with a large hooked nose, flowing
hair and beard turning white and sharp grey eyes, he was
the all-powerful general of a fast-growing army.

'I stood in awe of him,' Catherine remembers. 'I
wouldn't say I was frightened of him but I was a bit in
awe of him. It was very important to my father to know
that when he, the old General, was at home, one of us, the
grandchildren, had been over to see him. He lived just
nearby. And I can remember one day the awful feeling of
guilt and misery that came over me when I heard my
father's step coming into the house and realized that
nobody had been to see him. I jumped out of the dining-
room window—it wasn't very steep—and rushed through
our garden, so that when my father came in I, Catherine,
was at Grandpa's house. I couldn't bear the thought that
he should be disappointed and that my father should say,
"Oh, I do think one of you might have remembered for my
sake." He used to say something like that. It went into my
heart. And it associated my grandfather with a duty. Every
day that he was at home someone ought to go over and see
him. He liked to talk to us and he questioned us about the
corps and took an interest in our doings and in our pets.
He was fond of children, I think.

'One day he was questioning me as usual about how
Sunday had gone at the corps in Barnet where we were all
soldiers. Well, did you do this and that and the other and

did anyone come to the penitent-form? And we had to tell him about it. As it happened that day I had sung a solo, even though I had no voice. And he asked me, "How did it go?" I said, "Well, Grandpa, I did my best." . . . . "Your best!" he roared in his preaching voice. "Your best! What's the good of that? Your best won't be any good to the Army and the sinning world. Anybody can do their best." I could have burst out crying; it frightened me. But then, whether he saw the change in me I don't know, he went into his loving voice and said, "Darling, don't you see that's the

General William Booth greeting children on one of his motorcades.

difference between having God by the Holy Spirit to help you and just doing what you can do? What you can do is no good to anybody, anybody can do their best at something. You are going to rely upon the help of God. And you're going to be able to do better than your best." He gave me a little preachment, you see, which was quite precious to me and has been all my life.

'But he was really very good with children. He was very

fond of children and if he were home, which from our standpoint was very rare, at Christmas-time he always gave us a magnificent Christmas treat. Tea with cakes of every kind, more than you could eat, and a lot of fun. We finished up with singing. My brother, my youngest brother, when he was in his eighties still remembered the joy that filled him when he was ten or eleven and the Christmas present for him was his first army cap.

'On Christmas morning, it was always understood and we did it very faithfully that we, the children, went over to his house—it was quite near to us through our garden and across the road—and sang carols outside his bedroom door between about seven o'clock and half past. Well, one dreadful morning we forgot he was at home; we were busy with our stockings, I suppose. At any rate we didn't know anything until we heard a tremendous voice—he had a very good singing voice—shouting from our hall, which was a hollow and went right up to the nursery at the top of the house, "Christians Awake! Salute the happy morn!" We'd forgotten to go to him singing carols so he came to us as a joke.

' "Christians Awake! Salute the happy morn!" Oh, I remember it now and the awful feeling that went through us to think we'd forgotten him. So afraid that he'd be hurt. Oh, the troubles that loomed so large in youth. That was one of them. He was in a way a burden to us because it was such a dreadful thing to forget him.

'When he came to see us at our house it was a very special occasion. If he happened to be at home on a Sunday and my father was at home too, then, instead of our going over to tea with him, he came to tea with us. They used to sit next to each other, and I can see them now as if they were a cinematograph: their different changes of expression and their laughter and pouring out their worries and always talking about the Army. Every now and then Grandpa had a phrase, and I didn't know what it meant. He used to say, "small beer, Bramwell, very small beer", and I thought: what on earth does he mean, small beer?

'As they talked we would hope to be forgotten. Your only chance of being allowed to stay was to be forgotten;

otherwise they would say, "children, you go off". And not to be noticed you had to be very still. You were afraid to eat anything, in case you missed any of their conversation. They were quite open in what they discussed. They talked about the Army but never mentioned people by name. That I remember: you never knew who they were talking about. They talked about general problems, the difficulties of getting suitable buildings, suitable officers and the money to run the show.'

The 'show' was an ever-expanding business. From 1888 the Army's work amongst the homeless began. Typically the work had its beginnings when the General spotted a need and launched himself whole-heartedly into the challenge of meeting that need. Late one December night William Booth had been crossing the River Thames by way of London Bridge. In the dim light he noticed dozens of men, women and children huddled together in the alcoves trying to sleep. They were just a few of the homeless and rootless of the capital city.

The next day he tackled Bramwell on the subject. 'Do you know that men sleep out all night on the bridges?' he demanded. When Bramwell replied that it came as no surprise to hear of it he was told that he ought to be ashamed of himself for doing nothing. 'We must do something,' the General said, 'Get hold of a warehouse and warm it and find something to cover them. But mind, Bramwell, no coddling.'

Within ten weeks The Salvation Army's first food and shelter depot was opened in the West India Dock Road in London. It could accommodate up to eighty of the city's homeless. A second depot was opened in Clerkenwell, followed by one in Lisson Street, and the work expanded rapidly. The General's thinking on the social problems of his age were set down in a book he wrote in 1890. The best-seller of its day, selling 200,000 copies, it was called, *In Darkest England and the Way Out.*

In an age when poverty was seen as a result of personal failure and not as an undeserved misfortune, the book was viewed as revolutionary. It outlined a systematic campaign to eradicate poverty. First of all, William Booth put forward the idea of the city colony, a nucleus of institutions designed to meet the immediate need for food, shelter and work. Secondly the idea of the farm colony was floated, where training would be provided in agricultural trades. Finally the plan for the overseas colony was put forward where the homeless and workless from Britain could find new life and new opportunities. The General asked for one hundred thousand pounds to turn his ideas into reality.

Reaction to the book was mixed. Some tried to deny the very existence of a submerged tenth within the population. The Lord Mayor of London declared that no one slept out on the Thames bridges, though his opinion was immediately challenged by correspondents to London's newspapers. An attempt to discredit the *In Darkest England* scheme by discrediting the Army was made. A committee of inquiry was convened to examine the Army's finances and answer the whispers that the General was lining his own pocket with the monies he raised. The committee reported in 1892 and William Booth was vindicated.

While the *In Darkest England* scheme did not come to complete fruition it was certainly valuable as a prerequisite of the welfare state in that it prepared the minds of those in power to accept means of tackling poverty which did not involve condemnation of the characters of the poor. Certain parts of the scheme, however, were put into practice. The network of shelters was established and work was provided, notably at the Army's match factory.

The matches were sold under the brand name 'Lights in Darkest England' and were made without using the dangerous yellow phosphorus which was normally used by commercial match-makers. Yellow phosphorus caused 'phossy jaw', an illness contracted by those working in the factories which caused acute toothache, loss of teeth and a rotting of the jaw. The Army's factory opened in 1891, employed one hundred and paid them ten to fifteen per cent more than the commercial wage. Eventually it became illegal to make matches using yellow phosphorus.

Salvation for William Booth [wrote General Frederick Coutts] always meant salvation for the whole man . . .

His cry that the poor had nothing but the public house was a protest against their social as well as their spiritual deprivation. In the mind of William Booth 'the sacrament of the Good Samaritan' was an integral part of the sacrifice offered for the redemption of mankind, only this was a sacrament in which God's people could—and should—actively share.

So it was not surprising that there was hardly a community need for which the 'Darkest England' scheme

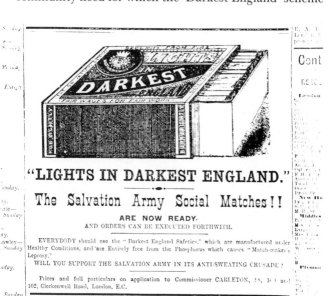

"LIGHTS IN DARKEST ENGLAND."

The Salvation Army Social Matches!!

ARE NOW READY.
AND ORDERS CAN BE EXECUTED FORTHWITH.

EVERYBODY should use the "Darkest England Safeties," which are manufactured under Healthy Conditions, and are Entirely free from the Phosphorus which causes "Match-maker's Leprosy."

WILL YOU SUPPORT THE SALVATION ARMY IN ITS ANTI-SWEATING CRUSADE?

Prices and full particulars on application to Commissioner CARLETON, 18, 19 and 102, Clerkenwell Road, London, E.C.

did not seek to provide. In pre-labour exchange days, labour bureaux were opened where employers could list their vacancies and men apply for work. A farm colony of some three thousand acres was set up at Hadleigh, Essex, which, at its peak, bred pedigree shire horses, grew grain and root crops, maintained several herds of red Lincoln shorthorns, more than three hundred white Yorkshire pigs and some eight hundred sheep, as well as about two hundred acres given over to market gardening and fruit orchards. A small holdings experiment was established at Boxted... A series of Samaritan posts—now known as goodwill centres—were set up in the poorest and most densely populated urban areas. Residential boys' and girls' homes were opened to care for those brought in off the streets or referred to the Army by the courts. Homes for inebriates (the nineteenth-century word for alcoholics) were established and, to the services for women were added mothers' and children's homes as well as residential hostels for young women.

While the Army was pushing through with its ambitious programme of social work, William Booth himself was able to call on the active support of his wife Catherine less and less. She was dying of cancer. To granddaughter Catherine this was the matter of which she was most aware, not the expanding social programme of the Army and the great stir caused by the publication of *In Darkest England*.

'*In Darkest England* I can just remember though I was very young. But Grandma was dying and I remember going down to Clacton, to the house by the sea. The house was hired as an officers' home of rest, but really it was rented for her to die in. She loved hearing the sound of the sea. I remember playing at her bedside. I had a little doll, about six inches long, dressed in pale blue wool, and she used to take the doll and perch it on her knee. It is my sorrow that I can't remember anything she said; you see, as she talked to the doll she was really talking to me. I can remember being taken and told she was dying. "Darling," she said, "you know I am going to heaven." I burst out crying. I was very fond of her. It was a curious thing because I didn't see much of her, but I was always at rest and happy in her presence. "I'm going to heaven," she said, "but you'll come, you know how to get there. Ask Jesus to take all the naughtiness out of your heart and then you'll come to heaven and we'll meet." She comforted me in that way.

'It was while she was dying that William wrote *In Darkest England*. Looking back on it I think it was a great solace to him, in between her bouts of pain and all the misery they went through because she was dying. It was a very

hard thing for them to accept as God's will because she
had become so important to the Army. She was a wonderful
preacher; she could get a congregation where William
couldn't and she was very sensitive about people thinking
that her preaching was better than his. It was different,
you see, made a different appeal. And to think that she had
to die seemed almost a contradiction of God's promises. I
can remember the gloom; my father suffered terribly over
it—all of them did. She had a wonderful influence on the
whole country.' Catherine's illness was long and painful.
To keep her mind clear she refused any pain-killing drug
except in the most extreme circumstances.

'Many times she thought death was at hand,' granddaughter Catherine wrote many years later.

> Bracing herself for the parting seemed to revive life in
> her. More than once she bade the family, 'take hands
> with me, I cannot get hold of all your hands, so Emma
> will be on one side, and,' turning to Willliam, 'you, Pa,
> the other . . . I shall feel I have got hold of you all till
> the light meets me. . . Love one another. . . Stand fast
> together. . .What does it matter what the world says of
> me? Not a bit, not an atom.' Looking from one to another
> she said, 'Oh, be not faithless; I have been so wanting
> in faith . . . If I had had more faith and been more
> courageous. . .' Tears flowed from her eyes. 'Have faith
> in God. Don't be afraid of the Devil. . . I am going into
> the dark valley believing.'
>
> At one of these 'partings' Catherine said, 'You who
> have joined hands with me, as we stand in the midst of
> this Jordan, there are not stones that we can set up as
> an altar but . . . promise me that you will be faithful to
> The Salvation Army . . . you promise?. . . all of you?' All
> respond. 'Say it one at a time that I may know your
> voices.' Bramwell first answering, she said, 'I gave you
> up to God when you were younger than your baby down-
> stairs, and consecrated you to be a preacher of holiness.'

All this time the General and the family went back and
forth to Clacton from their Salvation Army duties, all
except Emma and Marie, who remained with their mother.

She was still alive when The Salvation Army celebrated its silver jubilee, twenty-five years from the start of William's preaching mission in Whitechapel, though only twelve years on from the year the Army found its name. Fifty thousand people, including the six-year-old granddaughter of the founder, went to the Crystal Palace to mark the occasion.

'It was a tremendous day of marches and music. I was seated towards the front of the central transept. It was gorged with people for 'The Great Assembly', and a crowd, standing close packed, stretched away on either side of the enclosure filled with seats. I remember the sound of singing, people outside joining in the mighty volume that rose through the echoing glass dome as the meeting began. The crowds outside were not always singing in the right time and I remember them going on when we had stopped. There were Salvation Army bandsmen and singers and my Uncle Herbert leading a battle of song. It was a wonderful shouting time. They sang on the platform and then we sang from the auditorium. Wonderful, wonderful!

'There was a mountainside of faces towering up behind the platform. There was the glitter of instruments and a kind of dull roar as people rose to sing all about me. I remember the 'hugeous' band and what little sound it made. The brass was swallowed up by a different sound—a sound that seemed to fill the whole world, the sound of a vast sea of song. I shivered and felt like crying. There were movements, kneeling, rising and then, in deep blue letters on a white background, words began to creep across from one side of the orchestra front to the other: fixed high, and unrolling, a calico strip was drawn along, to be rolled up on the other side, so that one phrase was visible at a time. The silence was like cotton-wool. Sharp sounds echoed from far away in other parts of the palace only to make the near stillness more still. "My dear children and friends": the unrolling was stayed a moment. I knew who the words were from; I was one of the children. 'My dear child' was the phrase that belonged to my grandmother. Then the words moved on. There was another kind of movement, a dim rustling, an uncertain, sorrowful sound. Suddenly the

great building was full of it, as it had been of the mighty
sound of singing, only there were no verse ends. It went on
and on; it was not loud yet it filled every second with sound;
it wavered, fell, rose. Someone might scream and be heard.
I felt that anyone might scream. . . but no one did. Hand-
kerchiefs rustled and fluttered all over the mountainside of
faces on the orchestra, everyone was weeping: all the people
round me and me too. The words went on rolling, passing,
pausing: "My dear children and friends, my place is empty,
but my heart is with you. You are my joy and my crown. . .
Go forward. Live holy lives. Be true to the Army. God is
your strength. Love and seek the lost. . . I am dying under
the Army flag. It is yours to live and fight under. . . I send
you my love and blessing. Catherine Booth." '

Catherine Booth died on 4 October 1890. Her family was
at her bedside. The funeral service for the Mother of The
Salvation Army was held at another of the great London
auditoria, Olympia. One reporter commented, 'All classes
of society were represented. . . but oh, the poor! Never
before have I experienced so melting and harrowing a time
as, one after another. . . they recognized in the death of
Mrs Booth the loss of a personal friend.'

Thirty-six thousand people attended the funeral. It took
three hours for everyone to take his place. The lighting was
dim. The then new-fangled electric lighting was muted by
the fog which had drifted into the building. There were
prayers, readings from Catherine's addresses and, of course,
music. Not the great jubilant tunes heard at the Crystal
Palace but the sombre music of the Army's household
troops band playing the funeral march specially written for
the occasion by Herbert Booth, William and Catherine's
youngest son.

A white arm-band with a red 'S' surmounted by a red
crown was the only sign of mourning for Salvationists. The
meeting closed with an invitation to all who were willing
to make a whole-hearted surrender of themselves to God,
to signify it by rising to their feet. In all parts of the
building, one by one, hundreds stood, while the immense
concourse sang:

Just as I am, Thou wilt receive,
Wilt welcome, pardon, cleanse, relieve,
Because Thy promise I believe,
    O lamb of God, I come!

The march through the streets of London the next day to the graveside was four thousand strong. There had not been such a great funeral procession in the capital since the funeral of the Duke of Wellington. William followed the coffin, standing alone in an open carriage. His sons Bramwell and Herbert, mounted on horseback, rode either side. In the following carriages came William's daughters and Bramwell's little girls. They were in white and wore a white shoulder sash marked with a crimson cross and crown.

Despite the crowds lining the streets and the public solemnity of the occasion, to young Catherine grief was private. 'I was very much the child losing a beloved grandmother.'

William was sixty-one years old when Catherine died. He was to live another twenty years alone. For all of those years he was to devote himself to the Army and its causes. In the midst of the sadness surrounding Catherine's death he remained a fighting general. *In Darkest England* was making its great impact. But to his little granddaughter the book was not so important. 'It didn't loom so large. It was my grandmother's death which did. It cast a gloom on life, the fact that she was dying. I remember seeing my father crying. He was very devoted to her. Because her death made such a great impact, the fact that Grandpa was writing a book didn't seem important.'

When young Catherine was old enough she went with her grandfather on some of his tours. 'He took me with him when I was about twelve to sing. I only sang as a child. People like to hear a little childish voice piping away. I used to sing the song "Weary wanderer wilt thou listen", a song written by Commissioner Lawley, who also went with him.' John Lawley was one of the early converts and a great favourite with Bramwell's children. 'He had a wonderful voice and a great flowing enormous beard and he was a big man but could sing in the tenderest, most beautiful way.'

As early as 1904, the General as the perpetual innovator embarked on a motor tour of Britain. He covered over twelve hundred miles and addressed 164 meetings. The motoring general became a familiar sight, and Catherine, then in her early twenties, accompanied him on one of his West Country tours.

'He picked me up in Bath when he held three meetings on the Sunday, and on Monday we travelled to Bristol, where he was to meet the Lord Mayor. What struck me was the way, all along the route, people came to see him pass. I remember the extraordinary look on their faces. They held up their babies for him to bless and sometimes if there was just a knot of people he stopped the car and spoke to them, in a loving, fatherly way. He blessed the children. It thrilled me to go with him.

'He stood up in his special coat with braid on it and the peaked cap which he wore when travelling in the motor-car. Normally he wore a top hat. You see, all the clergy wore top hats. Funny to think how that fashion has gone out, isn't it, the silk hats and top hats. Everywhere as we went, every road was lined with people on both sides there to see him, just to see him go by. He'd got a great name, you see, in the country; he was known everywhere, William Booth.

'He was a very musical man with a beautiful singing voice and he had a way of helping people to sing. And he always had something special to say to back-sliders. People who had been in the Army, or in the Kingdom at any rate. I wish we did more now. If I were a leader in the Army now and was not so old, I should try to establish something, I don't know what I would call it, in every corps with a special responsibility to keep in touch with those who used to be in the Army. Never mind what they left for, whether they did wrong and were turned out, but keep in touch.

'We have a lot of private jokes in The Salvation Army and one of them began as a result of my grandfather's money-raising efforts. In his time at meetings where they were going to make an appeal and people present had

General William Booth and granddaughter Catherine on a motor tour in 1906.

perhaps not brought enough money with them to give, promissory notes were put on every seat. They would then write on them, "I promise to send the Army so and so", whatever they could afford. At one time these notes were made of a cheap yellow paper, and when the time came to fill up the note the General said, "Now you all have canaries, make them sing". That is, fill them up and send them in. It became an Army joke, and when one officer in Reading went to the Mayor wanting to gather a select company together to raise funds he said that he wanted to put a canary on every seat. The mayor was stunned with the idea that we should put a canary on every seat. He took it literally! You get a lot of fun out of life if you know where to look for it, and that was a bit. The poor Mayor! "What! a canary on every seat! How do you manage that?" '

In the years that followed Catherine's death, the general increasingly found himself at odds with his family. Much to his distress his second son Ballington left the Army in 1896 and Herbert left in 1902, as did his sister Catherine. The General's second daughter Emma died in a train crash in the United States in 1903.

Of the defections, that of Ballington was the greatest blow. He was in the United States at the time and left the army to found an alternative organization, the Volunteers of America. It was what he described as the General's 'despotism' which triggered the split. The old General made his farewell to his daughter with the words, 'I am your general first and your father afterwards.' Bramwell, his father's chief of staff, remained loyal.

Catherine, the granddaughter, was fully aware of the family break. 'If my grandmother had lived, I feel certain that Ballington, Herbert and Katie would not have left the army. They loved her so much and she drew them to the Army. She loved the Army's ways.

'And another thing: in those days there weren't the communications that we have today. Today you can pick up the telephone and speak to people at the other end of the world and it is as though you were with them, and they were with you. But there was nothing of that, only the letter and the telegram and the telegram was a great expense and didn't allow you to say much. The Army devised a way of sending messages in code to cut down the expense and there was generally a person at headquarters who had the business of decoding the telegrams. It was quite an important job. There was no other means of communication, whereas today if Herbert or Ballington had been at cross-purposes over something the General could have picked up the telephone and said, "Come over for the weekend, let's talk about this". They would have talked out of the troubles. Whereas letters took six weeks to come from Australia, for instance. In that time a lot could happen, couldn't it?'

Extracts from Bramwell's letters of the time, quoted by Catherine in the life of her father, illustrate the problems of communication.

> Ballington has not answered our wires. I long to see him somehow. Shall I get ready to go?
>
> I am feeling today very much about Ballington. Surely he will come round. I wish I could have gone. Perhaps I ought to have done so. And yet if I had there probably would have been an awful scare here.
>
> We have received a telegram from New York this evening . . . this looks very bad indeed, at the same time I must say it is only what I have expected for several days.
>
> Now I want wisdom from God as to what I say in this War Cry. I feel deeply and irreparably wounded. How God is going to bring good out of it, I know not! But his thoughts are above our thoughts.
>
> I have had a dull pain at my heart all day. . . Hard work has failed to give me any comfort. I feel Ballington has made ship-wreck.

The General's last great public appearance was at the Royal Albert Hall in 1912, on the occasion of his eighty-third birthday. His granddaughter was present. 'I was an officer then. I can see him now. They made a sort of pulpit for him to go up into. He was practically blind then. He was a very courageous man. I will never forget what he said. "While women weep as they do now, I'll fight; while little children go hungry as they do now, I'll fight; while men go to prison, in and out, in and out, I'll fight; while there is a drunkard left, while there is a poor lost girl upon the streets, while there remains one dark soul without the light of God, I'll fight. I'll fight to the very end." '

The end was very near. A fortnight later he had an operation for cataract. 'My father had to break the news to him that the operation had failed and that he was blind. It was a dreadful shock. Then he said after a pause, "Well, Bramwell, I've done my best for God and the people when I could see and I shall go on doing my best without my sight." He went on preaching but not for long.'

In less than ten weeks he had 'laid down his sword'. His body rested for three days in the Clapton Congress Hall. Sixty-five thousand people walked past his coffin. Wreaths were received from the King and Queen, the American ambassador and the German Kaiser as well as many from the poor people of London. A service was held at Olympia on 28 August, and the next day the traffic in London was halted for the funeral procession. The acting Lord Mayor saluted the coffin as it passed the Mansion House. The General was buried at Abney Park beside his wife Catherine.

'I remember the thanksgiving service before the funeral. Of my grandmother's funeral I have only a dim picture but Grandpa's funeral I remember well. It was in Olympia and I remember the great crowd and the singing. Of course there were no amplifiers. A little platform had been built and flags were marched in with the coffin and the coffin was put down in front with the flags being held around. The first flag that grandmama presented to Coventry was carried by the Coventry colour sergeant. Then there were ten or twelve corps flags and those of headquarters and staff officers and so on. So there was a body of Army flags, very impressive, marching in from the very back of Olympia right down the middle. I can remember my father leading the song that went, "We're marching through Emmanuel's

*General William Booth's funeral cortège passing the Mansion House,
London in 1912.*

land and soon shall hear the trumpet sound. And then we
shall with Jesus reign, and never never part again."

'It's a splendid tune. My father started suddenly from
his rather strained attitude of sorrow, raised his right hand,
called upon the crowd to do likewise and led them in
repeating the refrain to the verse they had just sung. He
took hold of the crowd. You could have heard, as they say,
a pin drop. "What, never part again: no, never part again;
and then we shall with Jesus reign and never, never, never
part again." It lifts me up even now to remember it. The
sound of the singing and the people. It was a wonderful
moment. "What, never part again." "No"—a great
outburst—"No, never part again". Of course that's the
sting of death, the parting. It's not only the mystery of it,
it's having had the last word and afterwards wishing that
you'd perhaps said something different. It's a wonder to
me that people can go on living and being so carefree.
They're all, we are all marching to our graves. Sooner or
later we have got to come to it.'

4

Holiness Unto the Lord

'The first memory I have of my father is the great treat it was to get into bed with my mother and father first thing in the morning. I was about two and I laughed a lot. More specifically the first memory of my father is hearing him pray at family prayers. Generally he had gone to the office before we had got up and then my mother took family prayers. In those days everybody had maids. We had a nursery-maid and a cook and a housemaid, and they came in and all the children came together for prayers. My father didn't go to the office on a Saturday and then he led family prayers. He often took the baby, the youngest, on his knee while he read the Bible and explained the meaning of what he had read. Then I can remember opening my eyes to look at his face while he was praying. I thought I had done a very wicked thing to watch. His voice sounded different when he was praying. So I see myself now so clearly as I knelt opening my eyes and watching him. Now that's my first memory of him. I think that perhaps is what makes it so precious to me and it's such a grief that so many Christian parents don't pray with their children.'

William Bramwell Booth, the favourite son nominated as successor by the General and founder of The Salvation Army, was a man of very different temperament from his father's. 'If the device on William Booth's banner was fittingly, "Salvation for the World", then on Bramwell Booth's should be inscribed, "Holiness unto the Lord".'

Catherine described her father as a mystic by temperament.

A little less energy; opportunity, in the shape of congenial surroundings: and instead of a man of action, earth would have counted one more dreamer among her sons, a dreamer whose dreams would have been worth recording.

As it was, necessity drove him on to a battle-field, and the mystic was almost lost in the soldier. Almost, but not quite, for the two can survive side by side: and any who listened with the ear of the initiated might, from time to time, hear from his lips the voice of the lover whose love reveals to him the Presence of the Beloved outshining all His works as Moses saw the flame in the desert scrub.

This strain in him was at variance with the man of affairs he was obliged to be. He hungered for the wilderness when duty kept him in the market place. He yearned for quietness, for reflection, when leadership claimed his presence in attacks on the enemy, involving, as real fighting always must, excitement, swift decision, loss. This striving, venturing life asked of him a service which must often be a sacrifice all the more costly that the bent of his spirit was contemplative.

Yet this seemingly incongruous element enriched him, refreshing his spirit as a quiet, almost hidden stream, whose springs are sure, waters the pastures through which it flows. His Master's promise was fulfilled for him. In this life he received a hundredfold the visions he had longed for and renounced when he sacrificed solitude and leisure to the call of the hour. The business was never dry to him, nor the meetings monotonous, nor men 'ordinary': all were transfigured! To this man who would have withdrawn from men that he might the more clearly see Christ, it was given to discern Him 'in the midst'. He spoke out of his heart's experience when he said: 'Do not let us make the mistake of looking for Jesus in the empty sepulchre, and missing Him in the common earth-marked garb of the gardener.'

Bramwell Booth's life was one of turmoil, of anxiety, of bondage to work: there were times when he quailed under it.

From young adulthood Bramwell was his father's right-hand man. He was the ever-loyal counter-balance to the General's extrovert genius. In the General's old age it was Bramwell who often reasoned with the Founder, using a persuasion recognized as that of and inherited from his mother. Under the constitution of the Army Bramwell was nominated as the second General by his father and succeeded at his death in 1912. His tenure as General was to confound those critics who said that the Army would not and could not survive without the charismatic leadership of the Founder and his wife.

The Duke and Duchess of York with General and Mrs Bramwell Booth attending a Salvation Army Composers' Festival in Clapton, London in 1928.

'When my father was General we hardly ever saw him. He went to work so early and he was travelling such a great deal. My brother, one or other of my two brothers, went with him in his later life. So they saw a lot of him, but the girls didn't go.

'When he happened to be at home I had a chance to see him. He was very dear to me. He was a wonderful person.

He was different. I used to say sometimes that he was the perfect Christian. He was a loving heart and he cared about the people. He took it to heart that his father said to him, "Now, Bramwell, do more for the homeless." He had got them on his mind when he was dying. "More for the homeless and remember China."

'And my father was able to send a group to open the work in China and then when the war came, with one thing and another, they had to close it. What has happened I don't know. They say some of the Salvationists still survive in China, but you see we can't go into the Communist countries. They won't have us. So that has shut us out of many places we would have gone into by now.'

General Bramwell Booth had much work to do which his father had not anticipated. He was able to see the growth of The Salvation Army's work during the First World War offering comfort and sustenance to the troops in the trenches.

'I think of my father and mother and how they doted on one another. My father used to make me his confidante. "Darling, do persuade Mama to buy another frock. I'm tired of that old frock she's wearing." We didn't talk about costumes or dresses but frocks. I felt rather hurt because it was a frock I had knitted for her; I was rather proud of that jacket and skirt. However, that's how he used to talk to me about Mama. Then, oh the joy she had in plotting something, a pleasure for his furlough. Saving up the money all the year round. We would have a pony and trap for the fortnight that we were away. They loved each other. Apart from The Salvation Army, they lived for one another.'

The great sadness in the life of Bramwell Booth came at the end of his days. His departure from the office of General not long before his death caused pain to many who were near and dear to him. As a historian of the Army, General Frederick Coutts described the circumstances of his departure this way.

On March 8th, 1926, Bramwell Booth celebrated his seventieth birthday. There was then no retiring age for a General and his forward-looking spirit still sighed for fresh worlds to conquer for his Lord and Master. He had cause for great content that much had been attempted and much done. . . . There was only one shadow over this. No leader could live for ever. Who was to be the General's successor and how was he (or she) to be appointed?

Such a question never arose when, on August 21st, 1912 the sealed envelope was opened which contained William Booth's nomination of his successor. The mantle of William fell automatically on Bramwell. But on whom was it now to fall? As far back as 1886 the Orders and Regulations for Field Officers had laid down that 'the General must and will appoint his successor' but 'the succession to the position of General is not in any shape or form hereditary, nor is it intended ever to be so'. It was on this last point that concern, justified or unjustified, had begun to be felt, and this had increased as illness overtook the General so that he did not return to his office at International Headquarters after April 12th 1928.

In the previous October Commander Evangeline Booth, the General's younger sister, had presented him with a reasoned memorandum urging that 'it would be wise statesmanship for the General to abolish the present system of appointing his successor and establish a method for his election'. This, for reasons that seemed good to him, the General was unwilling to do. He would not waive the right, he declared, of nominating his successor. The tension heightened as by mid-November it was known that his condition was serious. A national newspaper even announced that he was dying. So it was that under the provisions of the supplementary deed of July 26th 1904, seven commissioners. . . addressed a requisition to the Chief of Staff, Commissioner Edward Higgins, asking that a High Council be summoned. Whether their action be judged wise or unwise, right or wrong, they felt this step to be necessary lest the General's nomination of his successor should extend the hereditary character of that office.

The High Council met at Sunbury Court on January 8th, 1929. Some days of discussion ensued. A proposal was made that the General 'should retire from office, retaining his title and continuing to enjoy the honours and dignities of the same'. When he declined this suggestion the High Council then decided by a secret ballot of fifty-five votes to eight that his term of office as General should now end. These proceedings were arrested however when, on application to the High Court of Justice, Mr Justice Eve ruled that the High Council resolution was out of order because the General (or his accredited representative) had not been given the opportunity of stating his case. Obedient to this ruling, the High Council met again on February 13th when the General was represented by Mr William Jowitt K.C. Medical evidence was heard, as was the testimony of two ex-officers who spoke in his favour. Again by secret ballot the High Council confirmed its earlier decision by fifty-two votes to five. The five dissentients were Mrs Bramwell Booth, Commissioner Catherine Booth, Colonel Mary Booth, Mrs Commissioner Booth-Hellberg and Commissioner J. Allister Smith. Immediately thereafter two names were submitted for the vacant office of General, and Commissioner Higgins was elected by forty-two votes to the seventeen cast for Commander Evangeline Booth.

Despite the signed medical assurances that General Bramwell was 'recovering steadily from a very severe illness' he was promoted to glory on the evening of Sunday June 16th 1929. As for his father, the traffic of London was halted as the funeral procession moved from Queen Victoria Street to Abney Park with the coffin bearing the motto of the Order of the Companions of Honour: 'In action faithful, in honour clear'.

Until the end Bramwell had held fast to the belief that for future generals to be elected would bring the decay of a general's independence of action, unhealthy rivalry and intrigue and the eventual disruption of the Army as an international body. He was too fast in his loyalty to his father and his wishes. He recognized his father's authority and believed him to have been divinely inspired.

Bramwell Booth's final illness was one of pain and anxiety. He was attacked by neuritis and his right arm became seriously affected. He had periods of depression and sleeplessness. He worried how the High Council might interpret the supplementary deed of 1904. Did his illness render him 'unfit' to hold the office of general? He lost weight and his sleeplessness became so acute that he could only sleep with narcotics.

From November 1928, his daughter Catherine recalled,

His spirit was mysteriously aware of happenings of which humanly speaking he knew nothing. 'Are we alone?' he asked his wife one Sunday evening. On being assured no one else was present he said, 'How is the Chief . . . has he called the High Council?' A few days later he said, 'Darling, these men will take advantage of my weak state and getting things into their own hands. They will end up by turning me out and upsetting the Founder's plan.'

At the end of December the doctors pronounced him well enough to bear the shock of hearing what action had been taken. It was decided I should tell him. I travelled down from Headquarters for this purpose. The journey no sooner began than ended, for hours fly to meet those who crave even a moment's respite. I felt that the words I must speak would be his death. How then could I speak them? It was New Year's Day 1929 and in the evening, soon after my arrival, my mother and I went into his room, our hearts steadied to the task. I kissed him and he spoke cheerily, told me he was 'on the mend': he had not seen me for sometime; then, looking steadfastly into my eyes, he said, 'They have called the High Council'. His words struck me like a blow: So God had told him! I could not speak. I nodded . . . a silence fell. He broke in, 'Yes, I felt they would take advantage of my illness. I wonder what they really think in their hearts?' Then question followed question. 'Where is the Chief in all of this?' 'What is Frost's attitude?' And the position was fully talked over. After some time my mother left us, and my father at once said to me, 'If I die, Catherine, remember there must be no bitterness. I forgive, you and others must forgive too. They want to change the General's plan, they must know I shall never agree.'

The last Army ceremony Bramwell carried out was the dedication of his youngest grandchild. It was performed in the sick-room of his Hadley Wood house under the flag which had accompanied him around the world. Following the decision of the High Council he was not even invited to contribute a message to the Albert Hall celebrations marking the centenary of his father's birth. Neither was he invited to contribute to *The War Cry*.

Fifty-four years on, his daughter Catherine, who carried much of the burden of her father's distress, had this to say: 'I have made up my mind not to go into the circumstances of my father stepping down as General. What good would it do anybody? I could only do it, in a way, by denigrating, attacking others, people who were my comrades. And God knows what I suffered, what we suffered. It killed him. But at any rate, there it is. My dear mother was so courageous and she wouldn't have anything said. She said, his last words to us were, "Darlings, forgive. I forgive and you must forgive", and she kept us to that in the early years. No word must be spoken in detriment to harm the work that was carrying on. We just had to live through it. It has been very difficult. Very difficult. You see, they sort of cast us out. A dear man that we believed in and who had a good position was reported to have said, "The worst of it is the Booths won't go." Well that was it. They couldn't get rid of us. We all stayed. It didn't matter if we didn't get promoted or didn't get this and that. We had a work which we could do and we did it. I think my elder brother suffered most. My younger brother became a commissioner and had great success. He was a great preacher and had crowds wherever he went, so that the Army grew and succeeded, you see. My father was always the same, caring about the Army and caring about the people. He was genuinely interested in people. That's a gift, you know. Especially in a religious leader's life.'

5

Hard Labour

When Catherine left home to train as a Salvation Army officer, the twentieth century had barely started. The Victorian era was over, King Edward VII was on the throne, but still many of the nineteenth-century attitudes remained. The place of woman in society was fixed. Her place was in the home: she had no business in the professions or public life. Women did not even have the vote.

In The Salvation Army, however, things were very different. From the moment Catherine, the Founder's wife, had of necessity taken to the pulpit and proved her worth as a preacher, the Army valued the talents of men and women equally.

From the early 1880s William Booth saw the need for good, practical training for his officers. He put his daughter Emma in charge of training women and his son Ballington in charge of training men. To begin with training consisted of a very practical seven-week intensive course. This period was increased to six months and eventually to two years. Living conditions were basic and hours long. If the recruits thought the training tough they only had the words of the General for comfort: 'I sentence you all to hard labour for the rest of your natural lives', he told one group of 'graduates'.

Life however was not without its lighter moments, as young Catherine discovered. 'When I was in the training college on certain days visitors could come up and one day the children came to see me. I call them the children, the youngest end of the family. Thinking it would cheer me up they brought with them my pet mouse. It was so lovely, a darling little thing, that I said I would keep it for a few days. I had a little cubicle to live in and I used to let it sleep in the hollow of my collarbone. We didn't have such tight collars as you see now. And once it woke up in class. It crawled up and looked round the corner. But the terror on the faces of the other people! Oh, how I did enjoy frightening them with this mouse. We were all sitting in a solemn class and then suddenly the others couldn't contain themselves either with horror or with laughter, when they saw the mouse looking round and then going back. I didn't get into trouble. Perhaps I got away with it being the General's granddaughter; I don't know.'

Memories of her training college days mingle with her memories of Edwardian London. 'On Sunday afternoon we used to meet the watercress-sellers, crying "watercress, fresh watercress, tuppence a bunch". They would shout their wares as they pushed a barrow with bunches of watercress all put up. Sunday afternoon meant fresh watercress! I got very fond of it. I can remember in the training college we had a highly-educated Czech student who became a Salvationist and was sent to London for training. He knew English quite well and in the farewell tea—every session of cadets had a sort of farewell tea meeting with singing and testimonies—he got up, held up a long string of watercress and said, "I've enjoyed my time here, I've learnt many things and I've learned to like to eat this grass." It was a great joke for us—eat this grass.'

At the age of nineteen Catherine's training consisted of a blend of practical work and study. 'We had a certain number of Bible lessons, lessons on the regulations, lessons on how to lead a meeting. One of the things we learned was how to stop someone whose testimony was getting too long without offending him. I can remember those little things. There were doctrine lessons as well. Then the practical side of our training was going to a corps and visiting the pubs and leading the meetings and so on.' Visiting the pubs was a standard Salvation Army practice and still is in Britain. Soldiers and officers go into the bars selling copies of *The War Cry* and generally befriend the drinkers.

'They used to say to us in the public houses, I remember as a cadet, "that old William is making a fine hump out of it all for himself". How I enjoyed having them on. "It's not you poor girls we would criticize", they would say, "you're all right", praising us up. We were there with our copies of *The War Cry* and I would let them carry on running the General down, saying that he got the money that was given to the Army. Then at a certain point I used to stop them and say, "You know, you're all wrong, I'm his granddaughter." "What! are you really?" "Yes." Then I used to go for them. It's funny how little things stick in your mind.'

It was Bramwell Booth who required each of his children considering officership to enter the Army Training College on exactly the same footing as the other cadets. 'The founder's children had all begun their work in some post of responsibility; each of us, at our father's desire, and rather to the amusement of the General, came up through the ranks. "Your father's notion, nonsense I call it", he said to me laughing. All except Miriam, who was stricken with illness on the day she was to receive her Commission, were corps officers for terms varying up to seven years.

'The loss of Miriam was a great grief. She was the third daughter and was taken ill having completed her year's training as a cadet and year's service as sergeant in the Training Garrison. Her illness lasted seven years. Borne with heroic fortitude by all who loved her, but especially by our father and mother, a mysterious and heart-rending sorrow.

'I grew up with the feeling that I ought to become an officer. My parents never suggested it, never said a word to me about it, but I knew that the time would come. I told them that I felt I ought to and then the Army had begun the training college and there it was. I couldn't help myself.

'My first post was at Bath Two Corps. It was a bigger corps than Corps One at the time that I went. Although some parts of the police were still hostile to our outdoor preaching I didn't come across it. I remember the wonderful opportunity to talk to people on the streets and to see by their faces that they had forgotten it was the Army and they were listening to me. I remember once talking to a crowd at one of our slum corps at Hoxton, part of London. The sun was setting and the sky went a lovely colour and I felt prompted out there in the open air to draw their attention to the beauty of God's creation. I don't know what I said but by degrees all the men stopped smoking, they took out their pipes and cigarettes, a lot of them took off their hats; they were all staring at the sky. Well, it's a wonderful feeling if you've got hold of a crowd like that and can say, or hope you're saying, the right thing that will awaken in them a desire.

'I didn't find public speaking easy. I remember the words of my father when I had had one year as a field officer in charge of a corps, "Cath, never worry if your knees are trembling, so long as the people don't notice it." I've many a time started my talk feeling like that; my knees were trembling. It didn't matter as long as you kept up your courage and the people didn't notice it.

'We had roughs at my corps. We called them roughs; they used to shout and disturb the meeting. But you somehow got to be friends with them and some of them really got converted. Commissioner Jeffries was the leader of the Skeleton Army, I don't remember where, and became a commissioner, our highest rank.

'We expected at certain meetings that there would be disruptions. As a young officer I had a very rowdy Sunday afternoon meeting. Sunday afternoon is a very difficult time for a meeting—people like to have their naps and one thing and another—but in my day we always had a Sunday morning open-air meeting, a holiness meeting, a Sunday afternoon open-air and what we called a free-and-easy, which is what the pubs, I believe, still call their sort of sing-song. Free and easy, testimonies, choruses and so on. I made the open-air meeting a little later than it had previously been in order that we could march about the town and collect the people who were being turned out of the pubs. The pubs closed on Sunday afternoon and we would sweep them along to us. They walked in front and shouted and jumped and carried on and of course the more they did the more they attracted others so that we swept a

Commissioner Catherine Bramwell-Booth in the late 1920s.

really good congregation in to the Sunday afternoon meeting and it took something to manage them.

'They said, "Oh Captain, we'll take up the collection", and there was a friendliness, there was a come-togetherness, the fact that you could come into the Army hall and pretty well do what you liked. They liked that and we learned to manage them and taught them to sing choruses, the sort of which the highbrows used to make great fun. I used to have a cutting from a newspaper making fun of the Army because we sang a chorus which the writer described as going on ten or twenty times. What a ridiculous thing to do! But of course they didn't know that most of our congregations in those days couldn't read. It was no good supplying them with a song-sheet or a song-book because they couldn't read it; singing the chorus again and again and again was a way of teaching a chorus in the hope that during the week, or at work, the words and the tune of the chorus would come back to them and have a message for them. The people who criticized the chorus didn't know that.

'I can think of one testimony in particular that I heard as a field officer. That was when I was beginning as an officer. It was the testimony of a man who drove a coal-cart with a pair of horses. They went round the streets with coal in sacks. It was a Monday night and he had been saved on the Sunday or Saturday night. It was his first testimony. I called him forward: "Come and give your first testimony." "How have you got on?" I asked. And he said, "Well, no smoking, no drinking, nor swearing"—pause—"and the 'orses know the difference", and he sat down. I like to remember that: "no smoking, no drinking, no swearing and the 'orses know the difference". It's wonderful the work of the Holy Spirit. Changing people in the twinkling of an eye.

'I used to believe in the old-fashioned habit of giving an early testimony. I didn't always encourage it but I did very often. When you had dealt with a person at the mercy seat and he prayed and confessed and he got the assurance that his sins were forgiven, then you'd say, "Now, go on, tell the people and give your first testimony." When people had just been saved they were willing to do anything. If you said "stand on your head" they would try. "Tell the people what's happened", I'd say, and they would get up from the penitent-form and speak. After they've once broken the ice, the terror of it has passed away, they're willing to give a testimony whenever the opportunity arises. I have found very often that people can actually be saved in a meeting.

'I have found people who have given themselves to Christ just sitting on their seat at a meeting. They wanted to tell the people that they had dedicated themselves and so they went out and knelt at the mercy seat as a kind of testimony. But that rarely happens. The point of decision is still a difficult one. I have heard people say, "Oh, I got the assurance as I was walking down the aisle", before they reached the mercy seat. Bringing people to the point of saying "I will" is a very important thing.

'Grandma used to say lots of people came out to the front, they came to the communion-rail in those days, saying that they needed more faith. She said that that was a mistake. It wasn't faith they needed, it was the willingness to be obedient to God's commands. That's what they needed. And that is true I think today. As I say, I've said before and I'll say again, human nature hasn't changed.

'If I felt I was not making much headway with an individual I didn't get impatient. I feel so sorry for people. I don't think when you're really in touch with them, if they've really opened their heart to you, that you get impatient. You feel sorry. Men, women or children. And you feel how blessed you are. I do, having had such a wonderfully joyful childhood. What wonderful people my parents were. They left us to our own devices largely. We roamed about the country. It was a strange and beautiful beginning to life.'

Whether he was with them or not, Bramwell held a great influence over his children.

An unwavering and gentlest love was part of himself. As children we felt it instinctively; it was easy to confide in him and as we grew to womanhood and manhood the liberty and confidence of our intercourse remained. Children, I suppose love their parents in varying degrees; Bramwell Booth inspired in his children an affection which seems to me quite beyond the ordinary. To please him was for us all the most treasured happiness. To please God first? Yes, but how blessed for us that there was no clash between loyalty to God and loyalty to father. . . .When he talked to us about Christ, told us who He was and what He did, we understood. We felt, and in reverence I say it, that our father himself was like the Christ he loved.

At every stage of my life he appears to me as understanding me and understood by me. Though our time with him was so scanty, he never seemed out of touch with or in any degree distant from the interests of the moment.

Everything at home was subordinate to the Army's interests. How easily we might have come to hate it! It robbed us of so much. . . and there were many things we must not do, nor have: 'it would not be Army'. But instead we loved it, and first at the corps, where all of us became soldiers as soon as we were old enough, and later as officers, we learned to regard it as our chief love. And it was he, our father, who inspired that love. The way he talked of the people and of helping them, the scenes he described, all made us feel we were needed; and he was longing for the time when we could help. Things were only worth doing if they would be of some use to The Army 'in the future'.

Time for intercourse with our father was rare indeed after we had taken up our work, but he was so near in spirit to each that in a very real sense he seemed to be at hand. To his sons in turn came the joy of serving him personally as A.D.C. His deafness made their presence particularly comforting and helpful.

From our father we learned a true respect for men, even the most degraded; he imbued us with something of his own undying faith in man's capacity for goodness. And with what delicate consideration he helped us to note their sorrow and poverty. One evening in a meeting where there were several rows of kneeling penitents he beckoned to his daughter Mary, in whose command the meeting took place. She went to his side expecting to be told to deal with someone; instead he said, 'Mary look at their boots. The state of a man's boots is generally a sign whether he is really hard up or not'. And pointing out one man, 'his shoes are very poor, go and find out about him. He must be helped'.

His faith was a rock unmoved in any storm. His love a fire that never burned low. When my faith has wavered, when intellectual hesitancies have clouded my soul's vision, when in the darkness of inexplicable sorrow even love to Christ has fallen faint, what I knew my father to be, the Christ my eyes have seen in him, could not, would not, be denied.

Catherine was thirty-one when the peace of Europe was shattered by the outbreak of war. It was a testing time for The Salvation Army. Individual soldiers and officers felt their loyalties torn between love for their country and obedience to the Army's internationalism.

When he was declared General, Bramwell Booth's first concern was to keep the Army financially viable. He felt, unlike most of his compatriots, that the Army had to prepare for a long struggle. But if finance was an anxiety, there was a greater.

War was a challenge to the Army's international unity. . . Men were swept along upon waves of heroism and hatred. Indignation boiled over in extravagant denunciations. Could the Army march on its way unhating? Not without risking being hated for doing it! There were Salvationists in Germany as well as amongst the non-combatant peoples, and the fact that the Army's headquarters was domiciled with one of the belligerents was itself a menace.

To uphold the Army's standards of international brotherhood now became one of his urgent cares. . . . Some of his own officers failed to appreciate how momentous were the issues for the Army as a whole. In the eyes of some he was a pro-German, and on the other hand his vigorous prosecution of plans for work among the troops and the supply of ambulances by the Army, manned by Salvationists, displeased the pacifists.

The General was particularly criticized for writing of the sorrow in German homes, of a German mother's loss of seven sons. He also deplored vulgar attacks upon the Kaiser; at the close of 1915 he sent to The Salvation Army world these words: 'Every land is my fatherland, for all lands are my Father's.'

A Swiss was put in charge of war work in Belgium. A special ministry to German prisoners-of-war was started. The Salvation Army looked after thousands of troops stranded in London on leave and worked at the front with ambulances and canteens. Much of the practical work, as popular as it was with the ordinary troops, was viewed with some suspicion by the War Office. The trouble was that The Salvation Army was 'so religious'.

In 1916 the General much hoped the Army would be able to do something adequate for English troops in Germany. At one time it seemed that his proposal would be accepted, but the idea of using German Salvation Army officers for the work was not approved. Another instance of England's slowness to recognize The Salvationist as super-national.

The General was able to maintain contact with the Army in Germany and met two officers during the war in Sweden. He wrote in his journal, 'Many of the best officers in Germany are much tried. But I think, from all I gather, we shall weather the storm. It may depend on how long the storm will last!' He wrote at the end of 1915 to his commissioner in Australia.

It will ever be one of the outstanding facts of our history that amidst the most awful conflagration of modern times The Salvation Army has been found everywhere going steadily forward with its own great work of reconciling men to God, spreading the influence of His Grace and His Law in the great empire of the human heart, and holding up the Dying Saviour as the Great Healer.

General and Mrs Bramwell Booth in 1925 with (l. to r. back row) Bernard, Mary, Dora, Olive and Wycliffe with his son Stuart. (l. to r. front row) Bernard's wife Jane with their daughter Betty, Florence, Bramwell, Catherine, Wycliffe's wife Renée with their daughter Genevieve.

One of the special difficulties faced by the Army was the unwillingness of the War Office to recognize Salvation Army officers as ministers of religion. It took much argument before they were exempt from civilian military duties.

Australian, Canadian and New Zealand officers, however, were able to serve as official chaplains, and many are the stories told about one Australian, big William McKenzie. He visited the sick, organized outdoor and indoor recreations, became the confidant of any man in trouble and even went trench-digging with his men. In Cairo he would go the rounds of the local bawdy-houses, drag his men out and send them back to camp.

In April 1915 he landed with his men at Gallipoli. In eight weeks there were six hundred casualties in his battalion; few more than four hundred were left. He had to identify bodies from fragments of clothing or blood-stained pay-books. 'War', he said 'is nothing short of insensate folly. It is inconclusive in its results and devastating in its ultimate consequences.' The story is told of how he heard a young soldier crying out, wounded to death. 'Padre,' came the faint cry, 'do you know a Catholic prayer?' 'I think I do, my boy', came the answer without the least hesitation. 'Say after me: God, be merciful to me a sinner. I lay my sins on Jesus.'

Fighting Mac went on to Europe and to Passchendaele and the Somme. He risked his life crawling through the mud to the places the burial-parties could not reach to bury the dead and retrieve some identification of the body so that he could write to relatives. The horrors of war were to haunt him for the remaining thirty years of his life. He suffered from incessant nightmares.

As the war came to an end The Salvation Army looked ahead to the problems of peace; the poverty in the defeated Germany in particular. Reports came through of children being so short of food they were unable to walk and even too weak to stand.

His daughter Catherine recalls that the children's silent misery oppressed Bramwell and he grew impatient of governments. The newly formed Save the Children Fund gave the Army £5000 to spend on its behalf in Berlin.

Catherine was sent to organize the work. She distributed tins of milk and cod-liver oil. 'They were so eager to have the cod-liver oil. They had a dessertspoonful with every tin of milk. And to prove they had taken the milk themselves and not sold it they had to bring the empty tin back before getting a new one. I had the joy of organizing this work, which included a visit by an officer to the home of every child we helped.

'During the First World War I was in the training college. I was on the staff of the college. And during the war we had no men. The men's side was closed, but we had, sometimes, up to five hundred women. I was there as the second, and my responsibility was to interview each of the cadets separately. To try to win her if I thought, as sometimes happened, that I was going to have an awkward one, I would stoke up my office fire and we would talk, not during the working day but in the evening. I'd say, "Come in and we'll have a little chat." Very informal, you see. And then you would start. You had to win their confidence before they'd really open their hearts to you. It's a difficult kind of work.

'The type of people coming forward for officer training were mostly working-class. What we used to call, we dare not now, dare we, working-class people. Many of them had such wonderful stories. One of my stock questions was "When did you decide that you ought to be a Salvation Army officer?" It was a hard life, harder than it is now. And I was amazed how many of them decided as children of twelve, thirteen, fourteen. "I decided then, on such and such an occasion, and after that I did everything to prepare myself", they would say, "for being an officer."

"One of the frequent subjects raised at these informal chats was the cadet's own sense of insufficiency. You see, the more the training college opens up the opportunities and we begin to work at what sort of talkers they'll be, the more frightened they can get. "I'll never be a good talker", they'd say, and so on. I reasoned with them and chiefly helped them out of my own experience. I could say to them that nobody came to the responsibilities more naturally unqualified than I was. I had been a shy, shrinking child,

I was a shy, shrinking adult, and the public work was a torture, a positive torture. But I had to face it. And then I'd say to the cadet: "so will you".

'I felt obliged to face this public work not because I was a Booth, but because every Salvation Army officer has to face it. It was a torture, especially for the women, because of all the prejudice there was. Of course, now things have changed very much. I feel a bit anxious. But it's no good trying to do God's work for him. What God wants the Army to be he will prompt and inspire in the people. It's no good my hanging on to my old-fashioned ideas. In my day the woman captain went in to the district allocated to her with its soldiers, a rota of meetings, all the responsibilities of preaching, burying people, marrying people, dedicating the children—which is what we do instead of baptism—and it was a great responsibility.

'As an officer working and helping people directly I had sad moments. And perhaps that is what has reconciled me to not marrying. I don't really regret it now. But it is a wonderful thing to have a message for people who need comfort, especially after a death, which is such a dark, mysterious thing, and then to be able to bring them into the light, into the comfort of the thought, which if you take the Scriptures is very clear, that Christ gives us eternal life—whatever that means. I'm not sure what it means. There's very little told us, is there? People don't understand and some of them reject heaven, thinking of it as strumming on a harp all night. Their vision of heaven is so limited.

'It was wonderful to live in the expectation of being able to meet people and help them by talking to them and praying with them.'

Did Catherine ever have moments of doubt or questioning? 'Oh, I had questioning all my life in a way. I do now. The devil knows how to attack me. By nature I'm an unbeliever. Every now and then it sweeps over me; How can this be? How can that be? But the Lord Jesus becomes real and once he becomes real to you—you must excuse the way I put it—you can't get rid of him. Every time—there's Christ. He has got to be renounced if you renounce God. And then where would I be? I feel I put great importance on the question that the Lord put to the disciples: "Whom say ye that I am?" I feel that every person who hears about Christ, sooner or later, comes up to that question. Who is He?'

6

A Kaleidoscope of Memories

Commissioner Catherine's years as a Salvation Army officer are a kaleidoscope of memories. Her work was divided into three main areas, teaching and counselling cadets at the training college, working in the women's social-work field in Britain and being the Army's main liaison among Salvationists in the various European countries.

'I took a special interest in drunkards after my experience as a child in the Band of Love when I went visiting a boy blown up with dropsy and heard how his father drank and how families face such anguish when there's a drunkard. At the training college, when interviewing cadets, many of them said to me, "You don't know what our family owes to the Army, Major; you see, my father used to be a drunkard and we used to listen to him and could tell by the way he was shouting or singing that he was drunk and used to hide under our beds." They used to tell me how they suffered from either mother's or father's drinking. It's a fearful curse, you know, and still is. I wish I had the power or were a person of importance and could write to the BBC. I don't watch television much but I do listen. Everybody drinks—even in that harmless little thing, "The Archers", all about farming. That interests us a bit here. But every character drinks. I don't mean they're drunkards, but they all take intoxicants. I don't think that's a true picture of life, is it? At least I hope it isn't.

'A lot of people don't realize that the drink may get hold of them like a contagious disease. You get to rely upon it more and more until you're really half tipsy all the time.

'I can remember with joy some of the testimonies of

drunkards who had been saved and given up the drink. I'm thinking of one man now and can see the congregation. It was when I was in charge of the social work and I used to go to the big women's shelter that we called Hopetown. They had central meetings there and anybody could come in, but it was chiefly for the people who were lodging there. We had a special room—I don't know whether they still have now, and I'm afraid to ask in case the answer is no—prepared for the drunks with bedding in American leather over the pillows and the mattresses so that if people began vomiting it didn't matter. And one night a man and a woman came to the door. We couldn't take the man and had to send him to the nearest men's social, but we took the woman. Both got converted and when I went to the meeting in the hall at Hopetown, and it came to our time for testimony, this man got up. He was called Bob and he always came to the Hopetown meeting to give his testimony and sing a solo. They all expected it and knew it. I can see his face shining. He had been a terrible drunkard; his wife said they'd had five homes and he had drunk them all away. But we had given them a flat, a little flat in White-chapel. How romantic people are by nature! He used to go to his flat and ring the bell. The pleasure of ringing the bell and saying, "Does Mrs Roberts live here?" and getting the reply, "Yes, on the second floor". He would do it just to hear the reply. Then he went on his way.

'We fixed him up as a rag-and-bone merchant. When he died we gave him a proper Army funeral. I can see his march, a scraggy little march, going down Whitechapel High Street towards the cemetery. It was wonderful to hear his testimony. However simple, it was so different from a sermon.

'And then there were the young people in the police courts. They were part of our responsibility in the women's social services. Shoplifting they were charged with often—though that is the respectable name. Shoplifting doesn't sound very bad, but if you said, "She's a thief, she's up for stealing", then you've got the Ten Commandments behind you. Thou shalt not steal. Isn't that one of them?

'The Salvation Army is Love for Souls—caring about the

people, as my father Bramwell Booth said. Minding. Of course that was the power of the Lord Jesus. We ought to study more the words of the Lord. When he saw the people he had compassion upon them. That's what we need today, Churches, Salvation Army, the whole lot. Caring. Do you know how suicides are increasing—mostly young people? I think it's a terrible indictment. It's a judgement on our so-called civilization. The young with life before them. You can't bear it.

'I didn't go into social work until quite late in my experience. When I came out of the training college I was appointed to a corps and later to the women's social work. And then I had a break in my service. I was ill. I had a haemorrhage from both lungs. I think they practically gave me up. But I didn't give up—I got better. I was bordering on forty at the time, thirty-eight or thirty-nine.

'I remember the illness; it made a great impression on me spiritually because the fear of having to give up my work was a great grief. And I had to keep calm. All the doctors agreed I was not to excite myself or I would bring on another haemorrhage. I wasn't allowed to knit, even to read. For months I had to live a very restricted—almost like a cabbage—life. Lie in bed all day. Lie in bed all night. But contrary to all their expectations I made a complete recovery. And I can shout now as well as ever I could. I can take a deep breath. I was ill for two years; for the first year, at any rate, I was mostly in bed and in the second year I moved. My people sent me to Switzerland for the winter and then I came home to England for the summer.

'I had been a very active person and as I lay in bed I felt I'd followed God's call; in a sense, it sounds a horrible thing to say, but I felt it was God's fault. It wasn't my fault: I'd done what I'd been called to do and been prompted to do and I had broken down. I had known I wasn't much good at the beginning and now I knew it for certain. But I got well, that was the joy.

'I don't know what God's purpose was in allowing me to fall ill. You never know God's purpose. He never explains. That is what in my old age I have come to accept. Don't expect the Almighty to explain his doings to me or to you or to anybody. You see, God gives his commands and says, "Trust me—be obedient children, love the Lord thy God with all thy heart and thy neighbour as thyself. Live that kind of life and I'll help you." But he doesn't explain why sorrows come. It's one of the great stumbling-blocks in peoples' lives. Why should this happen to me—why should I lose such and such a one? It's very difficult to comfort them.

'These thoughts went through my head as I lay ill. I felt it was very strange. I thought I'd come to the end, but I hadn't. I went through some very dark passages at the time. I have all my life been a moody creature. But if you're not a moody creature, you won't understand what these moods are like.

'You have such ups and downs. Some days you feel you can face the world, the flesh and the devil single-handed. And another day you feel you're no good. Especially if you've had a disappointment with people. I've been praying for someone recently that I've been very disappointed in. I thought he was fixed to be a Salvation Army officer. I won't tell you the whole story, but say this—whenever I pray for him by name, then I'm tempted to feel, what's the good of this? What good can my praying do? I don't know. I don't understand. But I do know that I must obey the commands of my master. And Jesus said we ought always to pray and not to faint. Well, there's the choice open to me. Either pray and trust or faint and give the whole thing up. I can't contemplate that.

'And so when I was ill I wondered what mistake I'd made. At any rate, the joyful thing is to look back and say I got better and to remember the joy of returning to work. That's when they gave me the women's social work to look after and I remember at my welcome meeting I took the text from the psalm that goes, "This is the day that the Lord hath made. Let us rejoice and be glad in it." And I had a wonderful time helping people and doing things that hadn't been done before. Of course in those days we had thousands of girls and women, for various reasons, under our care.

'Sometimes I had breakfast with them; they didn't expect

it, you see. The message went round: Colonel—I was Colonel then—Colonel will take breakfast with you. They didn't know what was coming, I'd turn the breakfast into an occasion to talk to them and then in the end we had a mercy seat. We had a meeting really round the breakfast table.

'Many of the women came to us from the police courts. We had an officer in practically every police court. We were willing to take people instead of sending them to prison, so a lot of the young people, girls in their teens and runaway wives and one thing and another—we got them and it was a wonderful opportunity. Two or three months they were supposed to stay with us and they had to attend meetings and be interviewed by the head of the home—it was like an early probation service—and a lot of them got converted and used to come and see us and bring a husband and children. My dear mother, who really established the women's social work, had a beautiful scheme which she called "out of love". Those who had been helped, not necessarily only those that professed conversion, but many of them, were asked somehow or another to earn or gather a sum of money—three pounds I think it was—and that was to pay for someone else. She thought it would be a good idea for them to pay to help someone else. And then she gave them a Bible. Since we've been in this house I've had letters from people who say, "I still have the Bible your mother gave to me." I never went to the police courts myself. My officers went. I was the top dog and had plenty of other things to do.

'It was a tremendous struggle to get the money in those days. I had a great joy: I made friends with rich people, just here and there, and I would say, "Oh, we do want a new something. . .", whatever it was. Once or twice a particular man and wife gave me the whole thing. Gave me an eventide home. I don't know whether it's still open. We began then to do work for the old and lonely and to try to make them happy. I don't know if we always succeeded; it's very difficult to make people happy in an institution. Have you ever thought about that? I mean, you wouldn't like to live in an institution with a lot of other

*Commissioner Catherine (l.) at the Regent Hall, London in 1951 with her
mother Florence Booth.*

people very much the same as yourself. I went to one of our Eventide Homes once and we had a tremendous time. Some of the officers were horrified. We sang, "Daisy, Daisy, give me your answer, do". It was a mixed home—men and women: I found that they were happier together. For instance, the women paid more attention to their appearance if there were men in the home and the men were polite and considerate. It added something. They enjoyed it. "Daisy, Daisy"—there was no harm in it.

'Through the women's social work the main priority was to get the women, who were thieves and vagabonds, into a new way of life. In The Salvation Army we say, "Get saved. Get converted. Begin to please God. Begin to care about whether you please Jesus Christ or not. To believe that Christ died for our sins." I shall never forget going to one of our children's homes. We had a very successful home in Wales for boys on probation. We had a little farm and various things to interest them. I went to have a meeting with them and took as my text, "God so loved the world that he gave. . ." and so on and applied it to them.

'God gave himself for you. Amongst those boys, when I gave the invitation and said, "Now do any of you here want to give your lives to Christ? Come," we had quite a few out. I went down to pray with one of them—I used to do that, one or another in the meeting—and one boy, I should think about sixteen, was weeping his heart out and said, "Sister, I've never before understood that Christ died for me." Well, if you can bring that experience to only a few, it's a wonderful thing. "I never realized that Christ died for me." I can see his face now as he lifted it up, and the tears were pouring down his cheeks.

'I can't talk about my achievements apart from the group of women who were working with me, under me. We worked together. It was a beautiful thing to be able to say if a girl had been deceived—never mind how—if she was expecting a child, she'd nowhere to go, her mother didn't want her at home—it would be a disgrace—she could come to us, the Army.

'We had maternity homes all over the country. Thousands of girls came and had their babies. We had a section of the home with nurses and doctors where they went and had their children. My mother felt strongly that, unless there were special reasons why a baby should be adopted—like a very young mother, or something like that—to leave the child with its mother was the natural thing and that we, the Army, should do everything we could to help. We had a department to find suitable foster homes, so that they were able eventually to be together.'

Another job held by Commissioner Catherine was that of International Secretary for Europe. 'It involved travelling, which was a bore and an absolute terror to me. I'm such a bad sailor. More than once I have had to be carried off the Channel boat on a stretcher. But that is the way I had to go. There weren't any aeroplanes; they had only just begun. I came home from Norway for the first time in an aeroplane. It was wonderful—no sea.

'Everywhere I went I had to take officers' meetings. That was most important. You gathered together all ranks, all officers as if they were just brothers and sisters. It didn't matter what your rank was and I, as the visiting officer from London, would speak. Oh, I've had some wonderful weekends. Soldiers meeting on a Saturday night and all day Sunday, lectures about The Salvation Army in the afternoon, and a proper Salvation fight as we call it, at night, when we hoped to get twenty, thirty, fifty, a hundred people making a decision. You can't imagine it, if you haven't lived through it. What a joy it can be!

'I would go to a country and hear about how things were and maybe offer advice. I'd inquire into certain aspects of work. How they were doing financially, for instance. How they were doing with the number of cadets in the training college. That's a very important thing. I always went to speak to the cadets, however few. In Finland and Denmark we hadn't got many. In Norway twenty or thirty. But it was very important meeting with them.

'When the Second World War broke out one couldn't do very much travelling. I hadn't felt the war building up in Europe, especially as I wasn't in touch with the politics of the thing. I was concerned with the people who were drinking or stealing or the young folks who were unmanageable, and the war didn't impinge on it much—until it broke out and upset everything.

'A great many officers went out to work among the troops. It was a new adventure for us and we opened hostels in the cities where the troops took their leave. We provided a home from home for those who wanted to keep away from the bad parts of the cities. They could come in, have a cup of tea, sit about and read the newspapers—be at home with us. That was a good thing. It happened in Brussels, Orleans, Paris, Berlin, all over the place.

'During the war and at the end of it we did a great work. My darling sister Mary, the one who came next to me, finished up as a prisoner of the Germans, having been in charge of the work in Belgium. She visited the hospitals, sat with the lads and wrote home for them; and she helped many who were dying. Of course it was very heart-rending work, it took a lot out of her. Then the Germans put her in prison. Eventually she was sent to a prisoner-of-war camp. But she was able, wherever she went, to have a sing-song and to read the Bible. She had a way with her. Having been stationed in Germany she knew German and was able to reproach the guards who tried to stop her. "What! Germans wanting to forbid me to read the Bible! Why, you all read the Bible. The Germans I knew had the Bible. Can't prevent me from reading the Bible to my fellow prisoners!" And they swallowed it. Then she got my mother to send her some German New Testaments to give away. Some time later she went to an important meeting in Berlin and someone came up to her and said, "You gave me this when you were in such and such a prison. That's my testament. Now I'm converted. I'm a Salvationist." She had quite some adventures.

'When Mary was younger she had been appointed to Hastings, where they had a spell of rioting and people went to prison. She prayed all the time that she would be sent to prison—she thought it would be so good—but she never was. It was much later that she learnt what being a prisoner was like.

'It wasn't easy to maintain our work in countries that were at war with each other. In many places our work was utterly destroyed. You see, wherever the Communists went, we went too. I mean, they wouldn't have us. It was no good—you simply had to clear out and be thankful if you got out with your life.

'Our place in Berlin was for Germans, and in Brussels it was for our people. You see, that's the Army's business. Occasionally you hear it now in the newspapers: if there's a big fire somewhere The Salvation Army turns up with tea for all the men working at the fire. That's our style. Where there's a need. I think somebody invented that sentence—but it's too pompous—"Where there's a need, there is The Salvation Army." It's not quite as good as that but still it's bordering on it.

'During the war you couldn't get into Germany much. Germany came to grief largely. Dear people. I have been very attached to some of the Germans, splendid people: self-sacrificing, hard-working, proper Salvationists. Now they are revived in West Germany. But the strongest, most prosperous Salvation Army used to be in what is now East Germany. And we've been turned out there. Our headquarters was in East Germany. The large Corps halls and various things that we had going—that's all shut down. But now a niece and her husband are in charge of the work in Germany, where Mary was thirty or forty years ago.

'The Communists pushed us out, Hitler and the Nazis ditto. Yes, he didn't like us. What a strange thing. I remember seeing the films and hearing Hitler rave and the people cheering. What made the Germans sort of go off their heads to worship that man? It's extraordinary. Extraordinary. Human nature—queer thing.

'Working as International Secretary for Europe I travelled all about West Europe. The Army hadn't got anything going in Russia or Bulgaria or Hungary in those days. But I went to all the countries where the Army was at work and had the most wonderful opportunities to speak to huge congregations, sometimes in cathedrals, sometimes in churches, sometimes in secular places.

'But I wasn't cut out to do public work. I was a shy child and I have been that kind of person all my life. It was always an agony—this meeting or that meeting in prospect. What shall I say? I have got to get my message ready. But when you're actually speaking, when you have a congregation there and you can feel that they're listening, it's a wonderful experience.

'My public work was a tremendous burden because I never felt equal to it. But I had such wonderful opportunities to lead congresses and speak at important occasions. They really were a torture to me because I didn't feel equal to it and I used to remember Grandpa's words: "Do your best but count on God to help because your best isn't enough."

'I could preach in French and a few words in Swedish and German. I don't know if I would have the courage to preach in French now. The French are rather critical. They're not like the British. English people enjoy listening to the mistakes that foreigners make when trying to speak the English language. They quite enjoy it and give them good attention. But the French don't like their language murdered. I got to know Swedish fairly well; I can read it now. To say a few words brought you nearer to the congregation, but otherwise I had a translator and learned to speak for a translation to be made. Don't leave sentences hanging in the air. That's the great mistake people make.

'Once I was preaching in Helsinki and was translated into three languages. After each paragraph was spoken it was translated into Finnish, Swedish and Russian. Many Russians had come over from St Petersburg. There were four bonnets in a row on the platform. It is difficult to remember what you want to say next when you have to wait for so much translation.

'On one occasion my sister was preaching and used the phrase, "Someone lost his head". "But that's impossible, Colonel," the interpreter protested, "how can anyone lose his head and carry on running down the street as you say?" On another occasion my aunt used the expression, "It was borne in upon me"; the translator asked, "How can it be that you were born in a pond?"

'In other countries The Salvation Army has to fit in with the people and their preferences. But it is wonderful how close you become. The visitor from London can speak in a natural way to other Salvationists. I remember when I went to organize the distribution of the gift of milk for children which began the Save the Children Fund. I had the great privilege of going to Germany after the First World War. It was at that time that I went to Hamburg, where we have a secular hall. Our hall wasn't big enough, crammed full of Salvationists. The warmth of that feeling! The warmth of their welcome! All the miseries of war faded away and we were just friends and comrades. That's a wonderful thing and it happened to me in many countries. A feeling of oneness, that the people understood you.

Commissioner Catherine addressing a Salvation Army meeting at the International Congress in London in 1978.

'During the war Salvationists had been Salvationists. We met as comrades to encourage one another and there was always some special opportunity to speak about God and spiritual things because the people were more or less in grief.

'I can remember, at some of the great meetings we got up to a few dodges. Once at a soldiers' meeting in Stockholm—a big hall, full of people, a lot of them retired officers and therefore elderly people sitting on the front row of the platform—I was holding forth and I felt the meeting needed waking up. There weren't enough "Hallelujahs". Somebody once made that complaint and when he gave out the line of the song "Precious souls are dying"—"Hallelujah", said the congregation. Wrong place!

'Well, this time in Stockholm I thought the meeting was very quiet, it needed stirring up. A thought came into my head. I don't know how I brought it in—something about the wonderful inventions of the age. I said, "Now I can touch a button and—"; then I imitated an opera singer, with a high wavering voice, and the congregation rolled about in laughter. Afterwards they told me that the front row, where many had gone to sleep, had waked with a start and others were startled although they hadn't gone to sleep and wondered what had gone wrong when they heard screams from me. To master a congregation and to be able to make them laugh or cry and to reach their hearts with a message is a wonderful thing. I'm all against this modern idea that the sermon is outlived. Nonsense. If you have the right kind of sermon I think people come, ready to receive a message. Let them have it.'

7

Reconciling Man to God

The Salvation Army today is a massive international organization. In Britain it is enshrined in and protected by an Act of Parliament which not only sets out its constitution but also lays down the Salvationist doctrine.

We believe that the scriptures of the Old and New Testaments were given by inspiration of God, and that they only constitute the divine rule of Christian faith and practice.

We believe that there is only one God, who is infinitely perfect, the Creator, Preserver and Governor of all things, and who is the only proper object of religious worship.

We believe that there are three persons in the Godhead—the Father, the Son and the Holy Spirit, undivided in essence and co-equal in power and glory.

We believe that in the person of Jesus Christ the divine and human natures are united, so that He is truly and properly God and truly and properly man.

We believe that our first parents were created in a state of innocency, but by their disobedience they lost their purity and happiness; and that in consequence of their fall all men have become sinners, totally depraved, and as such are justly exposed to the wrath of God.

We believe that the Lord Jesus Christ has by His suffering and death made an atonement for the whole world so that whosoever will may be saved.

We believe that repentance toward God, faith in our Lord Jesus Christ, and regeneration by the Holy Spirit, are necessary to salvation.

We believe that we are justified by grace through faith in our Lord Jesus Christ and that he that believeth hath the witness in himself.

We believe that continuance in a state of salvation depends upon continued obedient faith in Christ.

We believe that it is the privilege of all believers to be wholly sanctified, and that their whole spirit and soul and body may be preserved blameless unto the coming of our Lord Jesus Christ.

We believe in the immortality of the soul; in the resurrection of the body; in the general judgement at the end of the world; in the eternal happiness of the righteous; and in the endless punishment of the wicked.

The Act received The Royal Assent in 1980—updating the Acts dating back to the old General's day.

The extent of The Salvation Army's work can be judged from The Year Book—a paperback of nearly three hundred pages listing activities ranging from helping prisoners to teaching disabled children and from offering help to alcoholics to running eventide homes, in 86 countries from Antigua to Zimbabwe.

The Salvation Army is at work in over 110 languages with more than 15,000 Corps. There are nearly 42,000 senior bandsmen, songsters number 65,000, there are 25,000 officers, 250,000 prisoners are visited every year, 150,000 police court cases helped, 18,000 people helped on night and anti-suicide patrol, 23,000 missing-persons inquiries undertaken with 9,000 people found. Salvation Army hospitals treat over two million patients every year, Army schools have 200,000 pupils, and Army hostels can accommodate 28,000 homeless or transient people every night.

The Salvation Army is also a publishing house, a travel service and a banking trust. It gives grants to aid the work of other charities including Help the Aged, Tear Fund, Oxfam and the Save the Children Fund. To rework an old saying: the sun never sets on The Salvation Army's empire.

In the hundred years since Commissioner Catherine's birth The Salvation Army has not only increased remarkably in size; it has changed from being a radical and controversial body and has become an established and much-loved institution. Commission Catherine and her sisters, although they have been retired from active service for many years, keep abreast of Army affairs through a network of friends, correspondents and relatives and keep up to date with current affairs through their radio listening and reading. How does the Commissioner now view the Army's work? Does she think, compared with the Army of her youth, that while it has gained in good will and official acceptability it has lost some of its punch?

'I do, I do, I do. I think we're too content to do the round, singing, reading, talking and, thank God, still inviting people to make a decision. But it is the pentecostals, the charismatics, the people who clap and shout a lot, who are doing what the Army used to do and they attract the people.

'The Army is becoming too respectable—and neglecting what was one of the foundations of the Army, the testimony. William Booth learned the value of the testimony in Cornwall, where he and my grandmother went as revival preachers. She wrote to her mother and told her how William had found what a wonderful effect it had if he began his meeting with the testimony of a man who had been converted the night before. And that is how the Army was, a testimony at every meeting. Now you sometimes don't have a testimony at all. Or what you have is quite out of place. You ask people to give their testimony and they write down a little sermon and get up and read it. Well, I don't call that a testimony.

'But so many Christians are inclined to be content. Even on the wireless now—I don't often listen because it so discourages me—the little babbling about nothing. Christian speakers should come in with a punch. You see, a lot of people today in our land, our land England that used to be the land of the Bible, don't know the story of Calvary, it means nothing to them. They don't know it and they don't hear it from the pulpit.

'It's a wonderful liberty the Salvationists have to speak to people in meetings. Sometimes when I have been speaking, or if I were leading a meeting, I have noticed someone in particular and have thought, if he should stay to the prayer meeting I will go and speak to that man. And then I find he's a backslider, and nearly always the grumble is that nobody has done anything, taken any notice of him since he left. The idea, you see, was in his mind that nobody cared. I think it's important that we should try to win back people like that. What an increase in our fighting force if we could.

'To arrest attention I think you need surprises. My grandmother said once, I can't remember when, that as an army we hadn't paid enough attention to surprise as a weapon. And now that's one of our dangers, we are drifting into a kind of. . .well, I don't know. I mustn't grumble; old people are always grumbling. They always think it was better in their day.

'I don't think people always ought to know what's going to happen in a meeting. I discovered that when I was leading meetings. I never stuck to a programme, which gets very dull, you see: song, prayer, song, maybe testimony, maybe not—that was the only thing which brought on what was often a surprise—Bible reading, invitation, Amen.

'As an illustration of this point I used to tell a story that I heard from a naughty acquaintance who named the person involved, which of course I never do. In the story this person was asleep, dreaming that he was leading a meeting, and he woke up to find that it was true. Well, there's a danger in going round the mill. Whereas a lot of people in the early days of the Army came to a meeting because they never knew what was going to happen next.

'Meetings could have been disrupted. The roughs disturbed them and interrupted the testimonies. Wonderful testimony meetings I've been in, especially, I think, hearing the early testimony of converts before they've learned the stock phrases, and they're really telling you how they got on. Oh I've heard some sweet things, beautiful things. And how the spirit teaches these people. You see, if only our people, the moment someone is converted, would get them to try and help someone else, perhaps to find out about the families—pray for someone in the family. Pray with people in the family and you don't know what will happen.

'Sorrows were poured out to me when I was in the training college. "Oh, you don't know what a difference it made when my father got saved: you see, he was a drunkard. We were all frightened of him, if he came home drunk", and so on. You get to feel it's a dreadful thing that the Churches, the religious people, don't ban the drinking—for the same reason that the Army does. Not because they're afraid that people here and there might become drunkards, but because they are anxious to protect those who have been drunkards. Anyone who has worked for drunkards knows that if they take a drink many of them can't resist the longing for it and they go back to it. So that we decided—my grandfather decided—there could be no drinking in order that we might keep our converts, that no convert might have to go to a comrade's house and be offered a glass of beer. And I think that's a jolly good reason. Isn't it? I have never, not even out of curiosity, wanted to taste alcohol. Somebody the other day, some press person said, "what! you've never tasted champagne?" I said, "No, I don't want to. I've never tasted it—thankful to say." And of course if you're thinking about drink, of course the women get caught in it more than the men do. The men are bad enough but the women are worse. A woman seems unable to resist it.

'We ought—and I mean when I say that, The Salvation Army—ought to be doing more visiting, as we used to among the people, so that those who are in sorrow can come into contact with someone to whom they can pour out all their troubles safely—not thinking about what impression they are making. It is a wonderful ministry, going to people's homes. If only the Church of England would wake up, because the parish priest has an entrance, he has the right to go into any home when there's a death or at any other time. If he could be the person who received the confidences of all the parish, what a wonderful opportunity it would be. But of course it's easy to find fault with other denominations.

'A lot of the people come from the Army to see me and we talk together and pray together. Sometimes I am able to offer advice to young Army officers. I say, work hard—that is how the Army was made, people worked incredibly hard—and care for the people. My father said, "The Salvation Army is love for souls", winning men to God. That's our business and that's what I say to the young officers. Visiting in the homes, preaching from the platform, talking to people at the mercy seat. In everything, what are you doing? You're reconciling man to God. That's our business in the world. When I listen to sermons sometimes I can't stand them; I think there's no bite in them. You know, they're eloquent and they go on so far, then—a sudden stop. No one is asked to make a decision, whereas no one will ever serve God without deciding to do it, will he?

'Is the Army becoming too respectable? I don't think we go out of our way to mix with sinners as we used to do. My mother periodically would get the Regent Hall band, march through the West End and collect all the bad girls, and they would come to supper with The Salvation Army. They came into the hall and there was not just a cup of tea and a piece of bread and butter but a jolly good supper—ham that they could cut up. Then someone talked to them and we had a bus ready to take those who were willing to come off the streets to one of our Army homes. I loved that work.

'We had in all the big cities someone we called the midnight officer. She worked practically half the night, talking. She got to know everyone on her beat, as it were. I heard a sweet thing about an officer who was visiting Bristol. She came across a woman who had been a prostitute who said to her, "Oh, don't waste your time on me, Captain, because I knew Captain so-and-so when I was on the streets in Piccadilly and I got all the truth from her and I'm ready to die. You go to so-and-so and so-and-so in the hospital. They don't know the way." Well, wasn't that a precious thing? I was never a midnight officer myself but I knew the women and was on the march. There's something thrilling about doing what they didn't expect you to do. I am a great believer in that.

'I made a speciality of raising money for the Army by getting to know rich people—especially when I was in charge of the social work. We would have a drawing-room meeting. Sounds very select, doesn't it? I don't think anybody does it now. It was held in someone's house and the lady of the house invited her friends. Occasionally I used to suggest two or three names of sympathetic people in the district; but mostly they were the friends of the lady who had lent us the house. I would talk to them about the Army work and explain and then, as my grandfather did, begged money from them.

'One of the problems for the Army today is that the motor-car has destroyed the open-air meeting. When I was working we could set up the flag and the drum with a few soldiers on any street-corner we fancied where we thought we would arrest the attention of a few people. But you can't do it now—the police won't allow it.

'The Army still makes music, and music is part of God's plan to make himself known to us. But the Army is making a mistake in fastening on bands, whereas it's the singing brigade which ought to be developed and they've been dropped largely. Still, I'm criticizing now: that's what old people always do, isn't it?

'But I feel that perhaps more could be done. We've dropped the solo. In my day you were almost no good if you couldn't sing solos. That was a great drawback for me—I hadn't a good solo voice, but I could sing alto. My lieutenant, the girl who was commissioned to come with me, had a beautiful, clear, untrained voice. She could sing solos. When we went to the pubs I played the guitar a little and then the people used to say, "Give us a song, Sisters", and we would sing a duet. I accompanied—and that was a help.'

It is not just the Army and its affairs which the Commissioner, from her vantage-point of years, considers and surveys. The events of the world in general concern her—its tragedy and strife. 'Poor world. I feel that the spread of Communism . . . Of course we're not supposed to talk politics. I don't know what your politics are and you don't know what mine are, but I think the spread of Communism is an anti-God spirit. They don't want God. Wherever Communism goes, then religion is shut out or crushed down, they try to silence us. Have you read any of Solzhenitsyn's books? I think they are very powerful.

(l. to r.) Russell Harty with Commissioner Catherine, Lieutenant-Colonel Olive and Senior-Major Dora during their 1982 television appearance on the Russell Harty Show.

'Every Christian leader should read *The Gulag Archipelago*, about his experience in prison. It gives you a very good picture of what Communism is really like. And it's a wonderful thing that a man trained in Communism—put through college in Communism, sent into the war and decorated and set up—becomes a Christian and sends a message to the old world saying, Wake up. It thrills me. He's in America; but do you know if it's true? I heard or read the other day that he lives in fear of being assassinated. Could that be true? I still shall hope that he is happy. I read Svetlana's book. She was Stalin's daughter and after his death wrote this very enlightening work. I think we ought to know, as far as we can, what's going on and be on our guard. The Communists have never come to leadership except by creeping in beforehand and then bursting out into a coup. They'll get us if they can. But this is a very wrong line for me to take: politics.

'No politics is one of the rules. And it works very well. You see, it would be a bit awkward if, say, you'd got a bandmaster who was a biggish man in the town and when there was a strike the men who were playing in the band were his employees. So no politics. Then it wouldn't matter on the Sunday that they were band and bandmaster.

'Poor world. I remember the day in 1945 when the first atomic bomb at Hiroshima was exploded. When I got the news from someone on the telephone I went into my mother to tell her about it; her lovely face lit up, a flush came into her cheeks and she said, "Oh darling, how wonderful." She was pleased. "It means the end of war." Well, we haven't had a war since—not here in Europe anyway. Though there has been Lebanon and many others in other parts of the world.

'I often think of my parents, two people who lived for each other, and then think what people miss today when they feel they can't bear one another and have to go in for a divorce. Of course, old people always know better—you know that, don't you? You must take all I say with a pinch of salt. But I do think that people rush into marriage today in a way that they did not in my time. Perhaps that is why I never got married, I don't know. But then it was important to be friends, to walk, as they used to say amongst the working people, walk out together, so that a man and a woman got thoroughly to understand each other's temperament. Then, I think, when it came to getting married, they were prepared more or less. Now, a few days, a little infatuation and they're rushing either to the church or the registry office and they're married. Then after a few years they're not married any more and they marry someone else. It's such a pity to spoil things. I think it's an awful thing for the stability of families that divorces are so easy and so widely tolerated. You don't feel ashamed of being divorced any more, do you today? It seems to me you don't. People even marry with the thought of divorce in their minds. "Well, if it doesn't work I shall get a divorce." And they don't stop to think of the effects upon the children, who don't understand all the ins and outs of it.

'It's terrible the number of children who must know that both mother and father have rejected them. And it is on the increase. What's a family without a mother, a father and the children? You see, the very foundations on which the family is built are being shaken. Better to keep out of it—as I've managed to do.

'I feel sometimes that I should have been so much in love with my husband, as my mother was with my father, that perhaps God couldn't trust me with a husband. He would have taken the place of God in my life—I don't know. Still, I should have liked to have had a husband and children. But I've had a wonderful life all the same. Full of joys and full of people to love. Often, when I'm praying I thank God that he has given me such nice people to pray for. My aunts and uncles were nice and now my nephews and nieces. I don't think I could have loved children of my own more than I love most of them, those that I have come to know well.

'It's a great pity that so many families now congregate in the cities. I'd like to try and change that or make the cities better, with more parks, more open spaces. But it would need money. Money, they say, is the root of all evil. It isn't, you know, it's the love of money. That's where the mischief comes in. To all the many people who say money's the root of all evil, I say: no it isn't, it's a great blessing, I wish I had some. But it's the love of money, caring more about money than about whether you do right—that's where the mischief comes in. Sometimes I think it's easier—though I shouldn't use the word easy, it's never easy—sometimes I think people are more likely to turn to God if they are poor than if they are rich. The rich are taken up with frivolous things; life goes by with nothing in it. Or so I see when I come into contact with them.

'There are people with advantages in life and those with

disadvantages, but I don't feel there is as much difference as people think. After all, what is God's purpose in putting us on earth? To develop man into the being, the kind of person God desires. To get his will done. That is just as likely to happen if you're among the poor—perhaps more so—than if you're among the rich. Still, all the same I wish I had a rich relation who could help me out of a hole now and then!

(l. to r.) Senior-Major Dora, Lieutenant-Colonel Olive and Commissioner Catherine with their father's portrait.

'I never wondered why some people were born into slums or had fathers who were drunkards. When it comes to the decision to acknowledge God, or not, which is the great object of even the slum officer, it doesn't matter why. It is no easier, in fact it is perhaps more difficult, for the rich to trust God, to be obedient to the will of God in their lives. To learn to recognize God's voice. You see, the great majority of Salvation Army officers are just very ordinary people; they're not highly educated, they're certainly not rich—and it has never worried me.

'When we were young it was a struggle for my parents financially and my father used to say later on in his life, "The Army will have the money it needs only when it has ceased to know what to do with it." '

8

Look Back in Joy

'It's a very strange experience, as I have said to my sisters, living so near to death as I do now. I know it must be next door, tomorrow, perhaps, or even today. But I don't want to die. That's another feeling. Ought I to feel guilty about that? I don't want to die as I'm in love with life. I want to go on living here where I've got the familiar things around me; the earth is so beautiful. Oh, it's all a mystery. I've been helped lately, just in these last years, months, by the thought that God never explains the mystery. Life is full of mysteries, we just get used to them and go on living with them, don't we? Christianity, the revealed truth as far as we have it, doesn't explain—does it? At least I don't think it does and you've got to get accustomed to accepting the mysteries that God imposes. Still, I am in love with life. I'm in love with the world and it could be so much happier than it is if people knew the joy of loving one another.'

The final chapter in Commissioner Catherine's career takes the form of an unexpected postscript. She had been retired for almost thirty years, living a tranquil life with her mother, until her 'promotion to glory' in 1957, and her sisters in Berkshire. She was of course in demand, as a preacher and public speaker, but her executive role within the Army had come to an end. She had time to write and the biography of her grandmother Catherine was published in 1970—a formidable work of scholarship for someone in her eighties.

Yet being a person of active mind who found that as the years passed there was no diminution in her mental activity, and who, though feigning impatience with her memory, was never impaired in her wit or judgement by its occasional hesitation, she yearned for something positive to do. 'I had a time of depression. I thought I was going to be asked to preach, speak at some Army function—but I wasn't. And it rushed over me, the thought that I was no good, too old, nobody wanted me any more. I stood on the step looking out on our lawn and had a conversation with God, if you can say it that way. "Help me to accept the fact of old age. It's your ordinance, Lord. I haven't got the physical gumption in me any more." The next day the telephone rang and it was the BBC wanting to come down and film an interview for television. They came and set everything up in this sitting-room, two burning lights, one on either side. Peter France interviewed me. Well, that was the opening of the door. The interview went all over the world and people's letters poured in—a great pile—telling me, many of them, of their former links with The Salvation Army—"My mother was a Salvationist" or "My grandmother belonged to the Army"—or pouring out their sorrows—"I've just lost my husband" or "I've lost my baby". It made me long for them.

'The broadcast opened up a new work. I've had boxfuls of letters and I have the help of a comrade officer who is an expert shorthand-typist. The Army is willing to pay for her travelling to get to me—her husband brings her in the car, he's an officer of course—and I dictate as many as possible. Or, I dictate the body of the letter then I add perhaps the name, if it means anything to them that I should call them by their name, and I add a bit at the end in my own hand. But even that is limited. Before I realized what was happening I got neuritis in my right arm and couldn't write at all. The moment I picked up the pen and began to write the pain went up into my shoulder. The doctor said there was nothing for it but to rest it. Amen!'

In 1978, Commissioner Catherine CBE received a somewhat incongruous award. She was elected 'Best Speaker of the Year' by the Guild of Professional Toastmasters and invited to a ceremony to receive the award, a rosewood gavel on a silver stand. 'It is quite probable', forecast one journalist, 'the toastmasters will not know what has hit them when Miss Bramwell-Booth rises to speak.'

'What nonsense! Toastmasters always urging people to drink and The Salvation Army rabid anti-drink. It was very funny. But the idea stirred up the press even though I said I never usually made after-dinner speeches. So, for the presentation the room was jammed with television, BBC, press people. They couldn't sit down. Well then, I thought it was the Lord—perhaps it wasn't, I don't know—but anyway as I looked at them I thought, surely

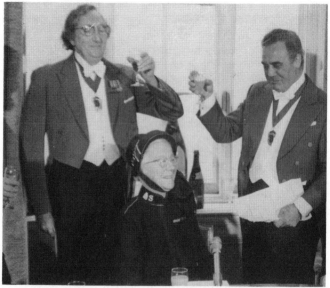

Commissioner Catherine voted 'Best Speaker of the Year' by the Guild of Professional Toastmasters in 1978.

it's the Lord's will. They're here and they can't get away. No one could get out without pushing through the others and it was an extraordinary opportunity. I thought most of them would be unbelievers as when I have seen journalists one by one and said 'Have you any faith?' the answer is usually no. So I preached to them and I don't think many of them liked it. It kept them there longer than they wished.

'I can remember some of the things I said. I complimented them. I said, "you're all clever in your own line, but if I were to ask you, I'd find you're doing without God." That sort of introduction. Then I said, "Some of you have tasted the wonderful experience that it is for anyone to love someone else better than they love themselves." They listened. Husbands and wives, wives and husbands, parents and children: I developed the idea a little. "So you're not only high up in your profession but you're in that wonderful situation of father or mother to your children and no one can ever take your place. God's given you that."

'Then I came to my point. I said, "Are you willing, you clever people who've succeeded, are you willing to think of yourselves merely as improved monkeys?" There was a horrible stillness. Nobody answered back; they very seldom do when I'm talking at a meeting, though I've told them sometimes I don't mind someone shouting out 'yes' or 'no', it brings us closer together. At any rate, that's the point: if you eliminate God you denigrate man to the level of the beast, and in fact he's worse because he knows much more than the beast.

'At the end a man wanted to ask a question. The toastmaster, who'd been very generous and warm in what he'd said, asked me, did I want to take a question? Did I mind? I said, "Oh no, I am hardened to them; everybody asks me questions, that doesn't matter." So the man came up, and there was a look in his face which made me think, now he means mischief of some sort. Anyway, he came up and stepped up onto the platform where I was sitting and said, calling out my name in a sort of exaggerated way, "Commissioner Catherine Bramwell-Booth, do you know that you have the gift of the gab?" So I said, "Oh yes I do, all the Booths have it." You see, I had kept him there against his will.'

Commissioner Catherine was also invited to appear as a guest of the leading BBC television chat show hosted by Michael Parkinson. 'Before the show someone asked me if I wanted to know the questions he was likely to ask. Well, I thought about it. First I thought, yes, why not, then I can prepare what I'm going to say. But when I started thinking I decided no, because I couldn't settle, you see. I might say one day, oh, I'll answer this way; then the next day it would sound utter rot. Wipe it out and start again. So I said no, I'd rather not know, and I went up not knowing. So many people wrote to me afterwards saying, "I did so enjoy your talk with Parkinson. You put him in his place." What did that mean? I wasn't aware of any effort to down him in any way. I didn't want to, there was no point; but this seemed to be the chief comment. "You put him in his place." Well!

'It was a curious experience. You're plunged into the unknown and afterwards you think of all the things you might have said. I did. He said at one of these talks, what a great pity it was that Christmas had become so commercialized and I think I answered him rather feebly. But afterwards I thought, what I should have said is that it's not as bad as the summer sales. At Christmas everybody's rushing to the shops—upstairs and downstairs looking at this and looking at that—and they're thinking about finding something to please somebody else. "What on earth shall we give old Aunt Catherine this year?" That's the difference between Christmas and the other sales, when people sit out on the pavement all night to be the first in to get a bargain for themselves. Everybody is thinking about somebody else; don't you think that that is rather precious? I'm sure it's good for people. Instead of thinking about themselves they're busy thinking about the children or the husband or the wife. No, human nature hasn't changed much, you know.'

In the summer of 1982 Commissioner Catherine was invited by the BBC radio programme 'Sunday' to contribute to a series entitled 'The Wisdom of Age' as one of several members of an older generation who could reflect on the experience of human nature gleaned over the years.

'Everyone ought to be concerning themselves with their relationship with God. That's the purpose of life. It was my grandmother who said, "Life is designed to show us that God is enough for us." I can't imagine my youth without prayer, without thinking about God's laws and answering the question that Jesus really poses—as much now as when he was on earth—when he said to the disciples, "Whom say ye that I am?"

'People don't have the advantage I had of a Christian upbringing. It's awful the way even Christian people neglect the spiritual life of their children. I met a director of a business, something to do with houses, and I was prompted to ask him—I don't always ask people—"Have you faith? Do you believe in God?" His face lighted and he said, "Oh yes, I'm a Methodist and we all go as a family to chapel on Sunday." I replied, "Oh, splendid. And have you any children?" His smile came back and he said, "Oh yes. Three lovely boys, they're all doing remarkably well at school and I'm so proud of them." I let him finish, and he looked so happy. Then I asked, "And do you pray with them?" A shadow came over his face and he said, "No . . . I . . . I . . . don't." Sadly I said, "Your three wonderful new spirits that God has trusted you with—fostered them with you as it were—and they've never seen you on your knees."

'To anyone I speak to who has had no Christian upbringing and sees no point in the Church or The Salvation Army I say, "You're only half alive, because if you ignore God you ignore the very purpose of your creation. What have you been created for? If you hadn't been created to please God, what's life?" That's how suicides happen. They're nearly all among the young, and increasing in nearly every so-called Christian land. What I mean by so-called Christian lands are lands like our own, and America, where people have the Gospel, the Bible, freedom and a certain amount of teaching, but are not Christians. It's more and more a secular kind of life. Look at us: we're breaking down God's laws one after another.

'We have a new gospel of material possessions. That's what it's supposed is going to make you happy: if only you were rich, if only this or only that, worldly things. But happiness is not there, even for the unbeliever. I say happiness isn't in the things you possess: happiness is in loving and loving is giving.

'It is very difficult to say I know how young people today

feel; I don't. I do believe that we're in God's hands. When people talk about the atom bomb, I don't agitate over it—I don't stay awake at night over that—because I am in God's hands. There's a certain rest in faith.'

Yet some of the events in the world the Commissioner admits do discourage her and worry her. 'Since I've been retired and have got no responsibilities on my hands, I can only pray, and then I do feel discouraged. I feel Christianity hasn't made way in the world as it should have done. We are so much taken up with silly little things that don't matter. People don't like us because we wear uniforms and call ourselves an Army. What does it matter what you call yourself? Then somebody else doesn't like the Baptists, because the Baptists say you can't go to heaven if you're not baptized. I don't believe it, but never mind, they do; all right, let them go their own way. Let all Christians be alert—shouting or doing something to attract the wicked. That's our business whether we are Church of England, Roman Catholic or anything else.

'Even in age I don't think one ever settles all the problems of faith. Some people might but I find the old fears and unanswered problems keep coming up. We live by faith. If we could understand faith it wouldn't be needed, would it? We shan't live by faith in heaven. People say to me, "You're so marvellous for your age." In my hundredth year I can enjoy so many things. I love life and want to go on living. I'm not craving to go to heaven. I find earth so beautiful and I'm now in circumstances where I'm surrounded by the things I love, trees, wild flowers, a blue-bell wood; I can see the wonders and beauty of God's creation.

'One thing I shall miss in heaven is gardening. I don't know; we shan't have weeds in heaven, shall we? You can't imagine how delicious a garden can be. I'm gone on gardening. It's one of the great losses in having lived to be so old. I can't garden as I used to; I haven't the physical strength. I have to pay a man to come in and prune the roses for me—and we can't afford to keep a gardener any longer. We have a cook, but what shall we do if. . .? That's one of the devil's favourite ploys: "What shall we do if?"

If she were to fall ill. When we came we had three indoor domestics, as well as people coming by the day, but now Madge who does our cooking is the only one left. It's all changed, hasn't it?

'I want to stay alive—but it's not through fear of death. It's a love of living and of loving. Loving is life. If you aren't loving anybody then life isn't worth having.

'We were all brought up vegetarian except for an occasional piece of fish. I think that's had something to do with

Lieutenant-Colonel Olive, Commissioner Catherine and Senior-Major Dora at their home in Berkshire in 1982.

our living so long. There are four of us left. I have two sisters and one brother. My youngest brother overworked, but he was in his eightieth year when he died. He worked too hard travelling and preaching, travelling and preaching. It's a very strenuous life. You can't get your proper rest at night. You're always in a new, strange bed and it takes you a little while to settle down; and then you're away to the responsibility of facing the next congregation. But of us four surviving we are all over ninety. Four people over ninety in one family—can it be some sort of record?

'I'm a conceited old thing and think I have an understanding of human nature. I've learned a lot about people, and what I've learned is that the human heart hasn't changed. I go back to my earliest days and people are very much the same. Suffering in the same way. The same things bring them sorrow and the same things bring them joy. Possessions, having a motor-car or a fortune, don't change the person much.

'Since I retired I have gone on being interested in people. But it is a very strange experience to be without work. I have been retired nearly as long as I was an active officer. I should never have retired but the Army rules retired me at sixty-five. Individual people still invited me to go and take Sunday meetings and I was writing, so I was occupied. I ought to be doing some writing now, but you see when you get to my age you sleep more and I have to rest in the afternoon.

'It is a wonderful thing that I can sit in this armchair and talk and without any effort on my part my voice is recorded and goes all over the world. Oh, I wish I could say something to stir up the Churches and denominations and whatnots to speak the truth and to call upon men, women and children to decide for Christ. In The Salvation Army we make a point, or we used to do, that children can be converted. William Booth was converted on his fifteenth birthday. He went to a revival meeting and I heard him say, "I made up my mind God shall have all there was of William Booth." Well, out of that, a boy of fifteen, came The Salvation Army.'

In addition to granting interviews to representatives of radio and television stations and newspapers from around the world Commissioner Catherine still finds time to help people on an individual basis. 'Even the other day, someone within our circle here came to me to talk. Her husband had dropped down dead at his work and even though she had been warned he had a bad heart she was absolutely broken up. It didn't make any difference that she was a

Roman Catholic—she had a faith. I had the great joy of seeing her in my room here; we talked together and she cried and talked about her husband. You see, people so often need to be able to talk about the one they lost. They cry over it. It's a time for weeping, but on the other hand it's much more agonizing not to be able to talk about things. She opened her heart and poured out her feelings about him: how they'd lived together and how they'd understood one another. It was all in the light of the loss, you know, that shines, that sheds a sort of glory on life. Then we prayed together. Afterwards she wrote me such a sweet letter saying, "Thank you for giving your time; thank you for what you've said", and it helped me so much, reminding me what a privilege it is, what a joy to be able to help people at a time when they need someone to help and lead them.

'I do believe that the Holy Spirit is a real person and can help us, prompt us. So that I don't worry about what shall I say, I feel it comes to me at the time and that it does come from the love of God. That gives me courage to speak the words or to ask the questions or whatever it is that I have to do. Nothing could be more wonderful than that people should know that you're the kind of person they can turn to. I heard only the other day of a boy who was brought up by an aunt who was very long sick, dying of cancer. She said to this dear child—I think he was ten or something of that age, round about ten—"Now when I'm gone find The Salvation Army and go and talk to them", though she didn't know anything about The Salvation Army really. I came to be involved in a roundabout way because someone wrote to my sister and said, "I don't know who to write to but because this dear soul told the boy he must find The Salvation Army, I must be able to tell him where The Salvation Army is." That's how I came to know the story. But that's a wonderful thing to establish such a standard in the world that the dying aunt felt if only the boy could talk to Salvationists he'd been comforted. Don't you think so? And that's one of the things you miss when you're old, you're out of touch. I am very sorry for that in many ways, but of course you can't keep up, you haven't the strength. People write to me now from all over the place: do come and do our anniversary, or will you come and speak at this or that? I can't do it any more.

'Oh, I've had a thrilling life, in a sense, when I look back on it. I'm out of the miseries, you see. When you're in it, then you feel it looms: the demands are so tremendous and you're such a weak, shivery person. If I had to preach in a cathedral, as I did in Bergen and in other places, I had an awful feeling, seeing the size of the congregation and the old building and all that. But when it was over I looked back on it with joy. That's how it is with my life. At the time I may have been in the depths over something, feeling I couldn't do it and I was no use. Now I look back and I feel, oh, wasn't it wonderful! How God helped me when my best wasn't good enough!'